Anti-Money Laundering Toolkit

Related titles from Law Society Publishing:

Anti-Bribery Toolkit
Amy Bell

COFAs Toolkit
Jeremy Black and Florence Perret du Cray

COLPs Toolkit
Michelle Garlick

Outcomes-Focused Regulation
Andrew Hopper QC and Gregory Treverton-Jones QC

The Solicitor's Handbook 2013
Andrew Hopper QC and Gregory Treverton-Jones QC

All books from Law Society Publishing can be ordered through good bookshops or direct from our distributors, Prolog, by telephone 0870 850 1422 or email **lawsociety@prolog.uk.com**. Please confirm the price before ordering.

For further information or a catalogue, please contact our editorial and marketing office by email **publishing@lawsociety.org.uk**.

Anti-Money Laundering Toolkit

Alison Matthews

The Law Society

ISBN 978-1-907698-58-3

Published in 2012 by the Law Society
113 Chancery Lane, London WC2A 1PL

Typeset by Columns Design XML Ltd, Reading
Printed by TJ International Ltd, Padstow, Cornwall

The paper used for the text pages of this book is FSC certified. FSC (the Forest Stewardship Council) is an international network to promote responsible management of the world's forests.

FSC
www.fsc.org
MIX
Paper from
responsible sources
FSC® C013056

Contents

Foreword

While it is fair to say that many firms have been identifying and managing risks for a long time, the demands of the Legal Services Act 2007 and the Solicitors Regulation Authority's introduction of outcomes-focused regulation mean that all firms – whatever their shape, size or location – must prioritise risk management.

Instead of adhering to a precise set of rules, the profession is now working toward a list of outcomes, supported by indicative behaviours, and this change in approach brings with it a greater focus on regulating the practice as well as the individual solicitor.

To help firms meet their legal and regulatory obligations, the Law Society established its Risk and Compliance Service a little over a year and a half ago. To date, the service's compliance support offering includes bespoke inhouse consultancy, webinars, monthly e-newsletters, master classes, seminars and conferences.

It is important for solicitors to be aware that they will not need to rework all their systems and procedures in the light of the SRA Code of Conduct 2011. This is particularly pertinent for sole practitioners, who are often the senior partner, law firm manager and risk professional rolled into one.

With these things in mind, the Law Society's Risk and Compliance Service in collaboration with a number of subject matter experts has commissioned this series of hands-on toolkits.

These practical guides have been prepared with the busy practitioner in mind. They aim to help reduce the cost of compliance for practitioners by providing a useful set of reference notes, definitions, best practice tips and templates. Much of their content is informed by first-hand information gleaned through onsite risk diagnostic visits and interactions with members of the profession, and in response to practitioner requests for tools to assist in their compliance journey.

Our hope is that these toolkits rapidly become 'must-have' elements in every practitioner's compliance armoury and to this end I recommend them to you without reservation.

The Risk and Compliance Service would like to thank the author, Alison Matthews, for her contribution to the Anti-Money Laundering Toolkit.

Preface

As solicitors act as gatekeepers for the financial and legal system in the UK, they have been specifically included by Parliament within the group of professionals required to take steps to prevent money launderers and terrorist financers making use of their services.

Solicitors should already be familiar with the Law Society's practice notes on anti-money laundering (AML) and anti-terrorism as well as the current legislation, e.g. the Proceeds of Crime Act (POCA) 2002, the Terrorism Act 2000 and the Money Laundering Regulations (MLR) 2007.

This toolkit is designed to accompany the practice notes and provides solicitors with practical assistance to implement effective systems and procedures to demonstrate compliance with their regulatory obligations. This is important given that chapter 7 of the SRA Code of Conduct 2011 (Code of Conduct) requires that you comply with legislation applicable to your business, including AML legislation. In addition, under the SRA Principles 2011 you are required to act with integrity and independence while upholding the rule of law.

Why have written procedures?

Written procedures will help your managers/partners, owners and employees to understand what is expected of them and so enable your practice to demonstrate to regulators and law enforcement that you are complying with your legal and regulatory obligations. Written procedures will also reduce the risk of your practice being abused by money launderers or terrorist financers. Written procedures help to defend your practice and your staff against regulatory, civil and criminal sanctions if your legal practice unwittingly assists a money launderer or terrorist financer.

How to use this toolkit

Legal practices are not required to use this toolkit, but may find it a useful reference tool to assess the quality and coverage of their own procedures. Regardless of how your legal practice chooses to use the toolkit, each practice should assess its risks and review and adapt the policies and procedures to fit the needs of the practice, particularly as many contain options for compliance. The risk-based approach means that legal practices should ensure that their systems work for their business and take account of the risks posed by their clients. There is no value in implementing systems that are difficult to use or which do not fit the business model of the legal practice. The support of managers/partners and employees is vital to the effective implementation and maintenance of AML and counter-terrorist financing (CTF) systems.

Legal practices may choose to use the toolkit by either:

- using some or all of the procedures and forms so their AML/CTF programme is integrated with their other business and regulatory procedures; or
- implementing stand-alone AML/CTF procedures which simply refer to other policies.

All of the draft procedures and forms in the toolkit are provided as Word documents on the accompanying CD-Rom. Simply purchasing this toolkit and putting it on a shelf will be insufficient to demonstrate to regulators or law enforcement that your legal practice has AML/CTF policies and procedures which are appropriate for your practice. One size does not fit all and you will need to tailor the policies and procedures to the risks faced by your practice so that you can show that your systems and procedures are relevant to your business.

You may decide that certain procedures or forms suggested in the toolkit are not appropriate for your legal practice, but consider whether they are designed to meet a legal requirement before deleting them.

Further assistance in meeting your obligations is available through the Law Society's Risk and Compliance Service: **www.lawsociety.org.uk/riskandcompliance** and its AML webpage: **www.lawsociety.org.uk/antimoneylaundering**.

This toolkit is based on the law, the Money Laundering Regulations 2007 (as amended) and the SRA regulatory requirements as at 1 October 2012.

Acknowledgements

My thanks to Emma Oettinger as this project simply would not have been possible without her fantastic support, advice and assistance. The profession is very fortunate to have her commitment, expertise and knowledge.

Alison Matthews
October 2012

List of abbreviations

AML	anti-money laundering
CDD	client due diligence
COFA	compliance officer for finance and administration
COLP	compliance officer for legal practice
CPD	continuing professional development
CTF	counter-terrorist financing
HMRC	Her Majesty's Revenue and Customs
IB	indicative behaviour
LIVR	limited intelligence value report
LPP	legal professional privilege
MLR 2007	Money Laundering Regulations 2007
MLRO	money laundering reporting officer
PEP	politically exposed person
POCA 2002	Proceeds of Crime Act 2002
SAR	suspicious activity report, also known as a disclosure
SFO	Serious Fraud Office
SOCA	Serious Organised Crime Agency
SRA	Solicitors Regulation Authority

PART 1
Setting the scene

This section of the toolkit considers how senior management can ensure the legal practice has appropriate and risk-based systems to prevent money laundering, terrorist financing and breaches of the sanctions regime.

1 Setting up systems

1.1 Which systems are required?

Under MLR 2007, reg.20(1), legal practices in the regulated sector (see para.1.4.5 of the AML practice note) must establish and maintain appropriate and risk-sensitive policies and procedures relating to:

- client due diligence (CDD) and ongoing monitoring;
- reporting;
- record-keeping;
- internal control;
- risk assessment and management;
- the monitoring and management of compliance with, and the internal communication of, such policies and procedures.

Regulation 20(2) of MLR 2007 sets out further requirements, including the need for policies and procedures which cover:

- the identification and scrutiny of:
  - complex or unusually large transactions;
  - unusual patterns of transactions which have no apparent economic or visible lawful purpose;
  - any other activity which you regard as particularly likely by its nature to be related to money laundering or terrorist financing;

- the taking of additional measures, where appropriate, to prevent the use of products or transactions which might favour anonymity for money laundering or terrorist financing;
- determining whether a client is a politically exposed person (PEP);
- the appointment of a nominated officer and reporting systems.

These obligations may be daunting as it may be difficult to know where to start and how to ensure that systems are sufficiently robust. The threat of criminal sanctions for non-compliance may concern legal practices that invest time and resources with the aim of 'getting it right'. This toolkit is designed to provide assistance.

Legal practices need to ensure that as well as effective policies and procedures, senior management creates a culture of compliance. Without the right culture, the legal practice will find it difficult to ensure compliance.

The key elements to effective policies and procedures are:

- management commitment;
- the appointment of a money laundering reporting officer (MLRO);

- the implementation of AML/CTF policies and procedures;
- the review/updating of existing systems and procedures;
- training;
- record-keeping;
- monitoring of compliance.

It is important to note the following:

- 'Management board' (the board) means the legal practice's governance structure, whether that is the sole practitioner, two partners who run the legal practice or an elected board.
- The terms 'MLRO' and 'deputy MLRO' have been used but some legal practices may have additional support from compliance staff or an AML team, particularly on CDD issues. In such cases, policies and procedures will need to be amended accordingly.
- Legal practices will have different approaches to business support functions depending on their size, but IT, accounts/finance, HR and marketing personnel may be able to provide valuable assistance and support.
- Legal practices should consider the points in each chapter and apply them in a risk-based and proportionate way given their risk profile, particularly their size, type of work and clients.

1.2 Management commitment

An effective AML/CTF regime requires the board to create a culture in which 'getting it right matters'. The board's support, particularly in terms of adequate resource, endorsement of difficult decisions and public acknowledgement that AML/CTF compliance is essential and that non-compliance will not be tolerated, is critical.

The board and the compliance officer for legal practice (COLP) must send clear messages to managers/partners (and owners) and employees that training must be completed (and on time), CDD must be properly undertaken and queries or concerns raised at the earliest opportunity. Building compliance into the annual appraisal/promotion process with the help of the HR team reinforces those messages.

Those responsible for IT, accounts/finance, HR and marketing are critical as their input will ensure systems work effectively, are properly integrated and are compatible with the other systems and processes within the legal practice. This will help the MLRO to ensure that the systems are commercial, practical and easy to use.

The board needs to be advised of major issues that could have a reputational impact, e.g. production orders or suspicious activity reports (SARs) to the Serious Organised Crime Agency (SOCA). The MLRO should provide the board with an annual report so it can assess the adequacy of the legal practice's systems. Ultimately the board and the COLP have responsibility for compliance and all relevant managers/partners can be subject to disciplinary or criminal sanctions if effective systems are not in place.

Support from key managers/partners sends the right message and ensures that teams, particularly those in higher risk areas, understand their obligations. Managers/partners can ensure that the systems are relevant and suitable for particular business areas. The pressures that all legal practices face, particularly in the current economic climate, are such that systems need to make compliance easy and improve, not reduce, profitability.

1.3 The MLRO

Under MLR 2007, reg.20(2)(d), the legal practice must have a nominated officer to whom employees and managers/partners must report knowledge or suspicion, or that they have reasonable grounds to know or suspect, that someone is engaged in money laundering or terrorist financing, if the information is received in the course of business in the regulated sector.

Under POCA 2002, there is no obligation to appoint a nominated officer unless you provide services in the regulated sector. However, chapter 7 of the Code of Conduct requires you to have compliance systems and to comply with AML legislation. Without an MLRO, it is difficult to see how a legal practice will ensure compliance with the legislation and the Code of Conduct.

Appointing the right person as the nominated officer or MLRO is critical. The individual must have sufficient seniority and the ability to command respect, access to files and other information, and a real understanding of a complex area of law to enable him or her to:

- convince the board, the managers/partners and employees to take AML compliance seriously;
- give clear, practical and commercial guidance;
- make appropriate and considered decisions;
- ensure that robust systems, controls and procedures are in place;
- arrange for relevant staff to have relevant training;
- identify when to report to SOCA and draft clear reports so that consent (permission to proceed with a retainer even though there is a suspicion of money laundering) is obtained where necessary.

There is no obligation for the MLRO to be a manager/partner, but non-solicitors need to have the support of the board so that they are credible. Once appointed, the MLRO should be in post for at least two years to provide sufficient stability and consistency of approach. The legal practice and the MLRO should consider succession planning so there is a seamless transition at the appropriate time. Appointing a deputy MLRO ensures that there is cover for absences.

While the MLRO has personal liability, the board, the COLP and the managers/ partners also have regulatory obligations under MLR 2007 and chapter 7 of the

Code of Conduct and can be subject to disciplinary and criminal sanctions if the systems are not in place or not working.

The board must ensure that the MLRO is properly supported and resourced, including the provision of systems, e.g. IT, and sufficient staff for the size and risk profile of the legal practice.

The MLRO must keep up to date with the legislation and any changes by attending seminars and networking groups, undertaking online training and reading relevant journals and regular targeted updates from the Law Society and other relevant associations.

Depending on the size of the legal practice, further support may be needed from a compliance officer or an AML team, who also need to be properly trained and supported.

The MLRO (and, where relevant, the AML team) must be accessible, approachable, pragmatic, commercial, supportive and sympathetic to ensure employees and managers/partners feel comfortable asking him or her for guidance.

1.4 Policies and procedures

The legal practice's AML/CTF policies should set out clearly the management's commitment to implementing an effective AML/CTF regime and outline the responsibilities of all members of the legal practice.

The policies must be relevant for the business and reflect how the legal practice operates. It is important that the policies are adapted to fit the legal practice so that everyone, whether manager/partner, owner or employee supports and complies with the policies.

The legal practice's policies and procedures will need to cover:

- risk assessment (see **Chapter 2**);
- CDD (see **Chapter 3**);
- ongoing monitoring (see **Chapter 4**);
- reporting (see **Chapter 6**).

In drafting your policies and procedures, the legal practice's internal controls will be relevant. Issues to consider include (see para.3.5 of the AML practice note):

- differing types of CDD requirements;
- timing of CDD, delayed CDD and restricting work until CDD has been obtained;
- exercise of discretion on the risk-based aspects of MLR 2007;
- use of reliance or outsourcing of CDD obligations;
- cash payments;
- reporting systems.

1.5 Review/update of existing systems and procedures

You must ensure your systems and procedures are fit for purpose. They need to be easy to use, sufficiently robust to comply with MLR 2007 and proportionate, particularly in terms of clients. They also need to be cost-effective and not slow down the client inception process. **Chapter 3** provides assistance on CDD systems.

Whether you are drafting policies and procedures or have taken over existing systems, you need to keep them under review and update them as necessary.

1.6 Training

Effective training ensures staff understand their obligations and raise queries or seek guidance at the earliest opportunity. **Chapter 8** provides further guidance on the relevant issues.

1.7 Record-keeping

Accurate, complete and accessible records will demonstrate that compliance is taken seriously and help to protect the legal practice in the event of an investigation by either the regulator or law enforcement. **Chapter 9** contains more detailed assistance.

1.8 Monitoring

If systems are in place but are not operating effectively, the legal practice will risk regulatory or criminal sanctions. Monitoring compliance systems effectively and documenting any corrective actions reduces that risk (see **Chapter 10**).

1.9 Using the toolkit

The policy (**Annex 1A**) and procedure (**Annex 1B**) attached to this chapter should be completed after you have completed the risk identification matrix (**Annex 2B**) and risk mitigation form (**Annex 2D**) in **Chapter 2**.

Annex 1A
Anti-money laundering, counter-terrorist financing and sanctions compliance policy

Purpose

This policy and the related procedures set out how [*legal practice name*] will achieve compliance with its legal and regulatory obligations under the AML/CTF regimes. All staff must familiarise themselves and comply with this policy and related procedures. Failure to do so [will/may] result in disciplinary action because of the risks associated with non-compliance, and may also result in criminal sanctions for the staff involved.

Application

This policy applies to all managers/partners, owners, and employees of [*legal practice name*], including those undertaking work through a consultancy arrangement, in a volunteer capacity, on a temporary basis or through an agency.

[*If you have any foreign offices, you should state here whether this UK policy applies to those offices as well, or if a separate policy applies to them.*]

[*If you have decided that certain areas of practice will not apply CDD measures to their clients, you should state here which areas of practice are exempt and from which procedures.*]

All areas of practice must comply with the procedures designed to avoid the commission of any money laundering or terrorist financing offences.

Money laundering reporting officer

The MLRO [and his or her deputy(s)] [is/are] responsible to the [partnership/management] board for oversight and implementation of this policy and the relevant procedures and for providing guidance and assistance to [*legal practice name*].

The MLRO is solely responsible for the decision to make SARs to SOCA and is the only person authorised by [*legal practice name*] to make SARs to SOCA [subject to any delegation to the deputy MLRO for holiday/absence cover].

For [*legal practice name*]:

- the MLRO is [*name*], [*email*], [*phone number*]
- [the deputy MLRO is [*name*], [*email*], [*phone number*]]
- [*list any another people with delegated responsibility for client inception/CDD obligations*]

Relevant legislation

Under outcome 7.5 of the SRA Code of Conduct 2011, [*legal practice name*] is required to comply with AML legislation and to have systems in place to mitigate the risks of our services being used by money launderers or terrorist financers. The following apply to [*legal practice name*] and therefore to all managers/partners and employees:

- POCA 2002 (as amended);
- Terrorism Act 2000;
- MLR 2007 (to the extent applicable to their area of work);
- all UK asset-freezing and sanctions regulations.

Principles

All staff must:

- conduct CDD as required by law and set out in the relevant procedures;
- monitor all retainers on an ongoing basis for warning signs of money laundering or terrorist financing;
- seek guidance from the MLRO [or AML team] on CDD issues or if they have concerns about a client or retainer;
- report any warning signs regarding clients or specific retainers in accordance with the procedure for making SARs;
- refer any queries or requests for information from law enforcement to the MLRO in accordance with the procedure for responding to law enforcement requests;
- follow directions received by the MLRO [or relevant deputy MLRO];
- maintain confidentiality;
- avoid discussing any potential or actual reports with clients or third parties unless authorised to do so by the MLRO;
- ensure they do not engage in money laundering or facilitate terrorist financing.

Responsibilities

Responsibilities of staff

All managers/partners and staff must:

- be aware of their AML/CTF obligations;
- comply with this policy and related procedures;
- undertake CDD on a timely basis in accordance with the procedures;
- be vigilant for warning signs of money laundering and terrorist financing;
- attend all training as required by [MLRO/training manager/*other*].

Responsibilities of managers/partners

All managers/partners are responsible for:

- including AML/CTF compliance in their file reviews and team meeting agendas;
- supervising their staff to ensure they comply with the AML/CTF obligations;
- supporting the MLRO [and deputy MLRO] in [his or her/their] decisions regarding AML/CTF compliance.

Responsibilities of [legal practice name]

[*Legal practice name*] is responsible for:

- appointing an appropriate MLRO [and deputy MLRO];
- ensuring the MLRO is given sufficient resources to enable compliance with the AML/CTF obligations;
- establishing procedures and systems to enable compliance with AML/CTF obligations;
- building a culture which supports managers/partners and employees in the implementation of AML/CTF policies and procedures;
- providing regular training on AML/CTF obligations to managers/partners and employees;
- reviewing the AML/CTF policies, procedures and risk assessments regularly to ensure they are effective and up to date;
- reporting to the SRA and law enforcement as required by law or regulation.

Confidentiality

Managers/partners and employees must treat information obtained as part of the CDD processes and any concerns regarding suspected money laundering or terrorist financing confidentially, even within [*legal practice name*].

If you have any concerns about possible breaches of confidentiality after a SAR has been made, you must contact the MLRO immediately.

Breaches of policy

Failure to comply with this policy [will/may] result in disciplinary action being taken and will be considered at performance reviews or appraisals.

Breaches of this policy may also require disclosure to the SRA, which may result in professional disciplinary action, given the obligations under chapter 10 of the SRA Code of Conduct 2011. As a result of a breach, a report may have to be made to SOCA or other law enforcement agencies, which may result in a criminal investigation.

Further advice

If you have concerns regarding a client or a retainer which may relate to money laundering, terrorist financing or breach of the sanctions regime you must contact the [*e.g. practice area partner, client inception team, compliance team, AML team, practice manager, deputy MLRO, MLRO*] at [*contact details*].

Related policies and procedures

The following policies and procedures must be considered when complying with this policy: [*amend the following list as appropriate to your legal practice*]

- file opening;
- staff disciplinary policy;
- annual appraisal policy;
- appointment and role of the MLRO;
- AML/CTF risk assessment;
- client identification and verification;
- ongoing monitoring;
- making SARs;
- responding to requests for information from law enforcement;
- exiting client relationships – AML/CTF considerations;
- accepting cash and monitoring accounts – AML/CTF considerations;
- record-keeping;
- AML/CTF training;
- monitoring AML/CTF compliance.

Glossary

AML	anti-money laundering
CDD	client due diligence
CTF	counter-terrorist financing
MLR 2007	Money Laundering Regulations 2007
MLRO	money laundering reporting officer, also known as a nominated officer
ongoing monitoring	review of retainers, including the source of funds, to ensure that they are consistent with our knowledge of the client, their business and risk profile
POCA 2002	Proceeds of Crime Act 2002
SAR	suspicious activity report, also known as a disclosure
SOCA	Serious Organised Crime Agency
SRA	Solicitors Regulation Authority
warning signs	features of retainers which may suggest that money laundering or terrorist financing is taking place

Date of effect/date of review

This policy shall come into effect on [*date*]. This policy shall be reviewed annually.

Annex 1B

Procedure for appointing the MLRO

Purpose

This procedure sets out how [*legal practice name*] will appoint its MLRO and any deputies in accordance with its AML/CTF obligations. It sets out the main responsibilities of the MLRO and any deputies and how they will report to the [management board/partnership/*other*] on the discharge of those duties.

Who is eligible to be the MLRO or deputy MLRO?

The MLRO and any deputy shall be of sufficient seniority to:

- have access to all client files, accounting records and other information;
- make independent decisions on whether to make a SAR to SOCA;
- make independent decisions on whether sufficient due diligence has been undertaken to allow a retainer to be accepted;
- undertake liaison with law enforcement following the making of a SAR.

For [*legal practice name*] the MLRO may be [*e.g. a senior partner, a managing partner, a partner, a director, an associate director, the chief operating officer, an AML lawyer*].

For [*legal practice name*] the deputy MLRO may be [*e.g. a senior partner, a managing partner, a partner, a director, an associate director, the chief operating officer, an AML lawyer*].

How will the MLRO and any deputies be appointed?

The MLRO will be appointed by the [management board/partnership/*other*] and the appointment will be recorded. The MLRO must consent to the appointment.

[*Number*] deputy MLRO[s] will also be appointed by the [management board/partnership/*other*] and the appointment will be recorded. The deputy MLRO[s] must consent to the appointment.

The role[s] of MLRO and deputy MLRO will be subject to re-appointment every [*number*] years.

The appointments will be recorded by the [management board/partnership/*other*] and the acceptance of the appointment will be endorsed by the MLRO or deputy MLRO[s].

What are the MLRO's responsibilities?

In discussion with the [management board/partnership/*other*], the MLRO is responsible for:

- setting the policies and procedures for compliance with [*legal practice name*]'s AML/CTF obligations;
- conducting the risk assessment for [*legal practice name*];
- establishing the AML/CTF training programme for [*legal practice name*].

The MLRO is responsible for:

- ensuring he or she [and the AML team] remains up to date on AML/CTF developments;
- deciding whether or not sufficient CDD has been undertaken to allow a retainer to be accepted;
- authorising the acceptance of a client who is a PEP;
- providing advice on AML/CTF queries;
- receiving internal SARs;
- deciding whether to make a SAR to SOCA, including consideration of whether material is subject to legal professional privilege;
- liaising with managers/partners and employees on the conduct of retainers where there are AML/CTF concerns, where a SAR has been made or consent from SOCA sought;
- liaising with SOCA and law enforcement where a SAR has been made or further requests for information or documents have been issued;
- liaising with law enforcement where a production order has been served;
- advising the [management board/partnership/*other*] on the level of resources required for appropriate AML/CTF compliance;
- reporting [annually/every six months] to the [management board/partnership/*other*] on [*legal practice name*]'s compliance with AML/CTF obligations.

What are the deputy MLRO's responsibilities?

The deputy MLRO will assist the MLRO with the discharge of his or her functions and will take on the full role of MLRO in the MLRO's absence, including making reports under the procedure for making SARs.

[Each deputy MLRO will specifically provide advice and assistance on AML/CTF compliance to managers/partners and employees in his or her designated [office/practice area].]

Related policy

Anti-money laundering, counter-terrorist financing and sanctions compliance policy

Glossary

AML	anti-money laundering
CDD	client due diligence
consent	permission to proceed with a retainer even though there is a suspicion of money laundering
CTF	counter-terrorist financing
MLRO	money laundering reporting officer, also known as a nominated officer
PEP	politically exposed person
SAR	suspicious activity report, also known as a disclosure
SOCA	Serious Organised Crime Agency

Date of effect/date of review

This policy shall come into effect on [*date*]. This policy shall be reviewed annually.

Annex 1C

Record of appointment of the MLRO

The [management board/partnership/*other*] of [*legal practice name*] at its meeting of [*date*] appointed the following individual[s] to discharge the role[s] of money laundering reporting officer [and deputy money laundering reporting officer(s)] [for the period of [X] years/until further notice].

Name of [senior partner/managing partner/CEO/*other*]:	
Signature:	
Date:	

Money laundering reporting officer

Name:	
Role in [*legal practice name*]:	
Signature accepting appointment:	

[*Delete the following if necessary:*]

Deputy money laundering reporting officer

Name:	
Role in [*legal practice name*]:	
[Office or practice area of responsibility:]	
Signature accepting appointment:	

Deputy money laundering reporting officer

Name:	
Role in [*legal practice name*]:	
[Office or practice area of responsibility:]	
Signature accepting appointment:	

2 Assessing the risk to the legal practice

Legal practices should already be familiar with the concept of risk management and the risk-based approach. Rule 5 of the Solicitors' Code of Conduct 2007 required legal practices to manage their risks. Outcome 7.3 of the SRA Code of Conduct 2011 requires legal practices to identify, monitor and manage risks to compliance.

MLR 2007 permit a risk-based approach to compliance with CDD obligations. It is not a new concept nor a zero-failure regime. By using the risk-based approach, you can target your resources effectively and demonstrate to the Solicitors Regulation Authority (SRA) that you are managing the risks in your business. You may minimise the costs of compliance and it gives you greater flexibility to respond to emerging risks.

Before setting up procedures or reviewing existing procedures, the MLRO, COLP and senior management should take the time to identify and document the AML/ CTF and sanctions risks which specifically apply to the legal practice. This can feed into the risk register, so that there is a coordinated approach within the legal practice to risk management.

When merging with another legal practice, taking on a new area of business or branching out into a new jurisdiction, you should re-assess the risks. When preparing the MLRO report to management (see **Chapter 10**), it is appropriate to review the risks applicable to the legal practice as at that date.

Issues to consider when assessing risk are covered in chapter 2 of the Law Society's AML practice note, while chapter 11 of the practice note explains some of the warning signs and methodologies behind the risk factors.

Having identified the risks, you can see where your gaps are and assess how to close the gaps and manage the risks. You will need to ensure your systems, procedures and training are up to date or that you identify what changes will be required. This information will feed into your compliance plan, which sets out how you will meet your regulatory obligations (see rule 8 of the SRA Authorisation Rules for Legal Services Bodies and Licensable Bodies 2011).

2.1 Using the toolkit

The assessment of risk is an industry in itself, with many books, courses and complicated tools aiming to identify, measure and mitigate all types of different risks. This toolkit does not attempt to make you an expert on risk analysis or cover all possibilities but does try to help you assess the risks for your practice.

The risk identification matrix (**Annex 2B**) sets out common AML/CTF risk factors faced by legal practices and indicates general risk categories.

The MLRO and senior management should discuss which of the risk factors are present in the legal practice and simply circle them on the form. You may need to add areas of practice, client types or jurisdictions. If certain types of clients only instruct one area of practice, then that should be noted. If the suggested risk category for a particular factor is not appropriate, you should document the reason why. The matrix can then be amended to reflect the risks present in the legal practice.

The purpose of the risk identification matrix is to ensure that the legal practice has a shared understanding of the AML/CTF risks faced by the practice and can take steps to mitigate those risks.

The high-risk country checklist (**Annex 2C**) should be maintained by the MLRO. This list, along with the completed risk identification matrix, should be available to employees either in the AML manual or on the legal practice's intranet. Employees responsible for completing the client inception forms will need to refer to these lists and all employees need to understand the sanctions regime.

The risk mitigation form (**Annex 2D**) should be completed by the MLRO and senior management to set out the high-level approach and resourcing decisions which are being taken to enable compliance. These decisions will then determine the options selected by the MLRO in adapting the remaining procedures and forms in the toolkit to the specific requirements of the legal practice.

Annex 2A
AML/CTF and sanctions risk assessment procedure

Purpose

This procedure sets out how [*legal practice name*] will assess the risks of being involved in money laundering or terrorist financing or breaching sanctions requirements.

Application

This procedure applies to senior management, the MLRO and the COLP.

Initial risk assessment

The [board/partnership/management team/*other*], MLRO and COLP will identify, assess and record the AML/CTF and sanctions risks applicable to [*legal practice name*] using [the risk identification matrix/*other*].

Taking into account the risks identified, the [board/partnership/management team/*other*], MLRO and COLP will complete the risk mitigation form, setting out how the legal practice will meet its regulatory and legal obligations.

The [COLP/MLRO] will ensure that this information is added to the risk register and compliance plan for [*legal practice name*].

Ongoing risk assessment

The [board/partnership/management team/*other*], MLRO and COLP will review the risk profile of the legal practice whenever [*legal practice name*] considers any significant change to its business model, including:

- merging with or taking over another legal practice;
- entering into a referral arrangement or best-friend relationship with another organisation;
- opening a new office;
- undertaking a new area of practice;
- seeking clients from a new jurisdiction or a new domestic market with links to a foreign jurisdiction.

The MLRO will review the risk profile of [*legal practice name*] during the preparation of the MLRO report to management.

The MLRO is required to keep the high-risk country checklist updated and ensure systems are in place to check whether clients are on the sanctions lists before monies are received from or sent to clients.

Communication to employees

The completed risk profile of [*legal practice name*] and the high-risk country checklist will be made available to all employees of [*legal practice name*] through the [AML manual/intranet/*other*].

Related policy

Anti-money laundering, counter-terrorist financing and sanctions compliance policy

Glossary

AML	anti-money laundering
COLP	compliance officer for legal practice
CTF	counter-terrorist financing
MLRO	money laundering reporting officer

Date of effect/date of review

This procedure shall come into effect on [*date*]. This procedure shall be reviewed annually.

Annex 2B
Risk identification matrix

Legal practice features

Feature	Risk issues to consider
Single office	• whether you need to have only one deputy MLRO to cover absences • whether simpler systems are appropriate, as consistency should be easier to monitor • whether to make use of external training support, e.g. to have access to sufficient case studies to help employees appreciate emerging or unusual risks
Multiple domestic offices	• having deputy MLROs for each office to ensure sufficient expertise is available to employees • the need to have more formalised systems to ensure consistency of approach • how management will have an effective overview of compliance across all offices • how you will deploy training effectively and efficiently
Multiple overseas offices	• different AML/CTF obligations in each jurisdiction and how you will transfer clients between jurisdictions • having deputy MLROs for each office or jurisdiction to ensure sufficient expertise is available to employees • the need to have more formalised systems to ensure consistency • how management will have an effective overview of compliance across all offices • how you will deploy training effectively and efficiently
Limited central support function	• who will undertake CDD and the need to ensure those employees receive frequent, detailed training on CDD procedures and warning signs • how you will ensure sufficient expertise is available to all employees • the need to have more extensive monitoring options for compliance
Full central support function	• where CDD is undertaken by a central team, you will need to ensure that employees see and understand the CDD results for ongoing monitoring purposes, while training can focus more on warning signs • the central team need to be trained in detail on CDD procedures and be able to provide advice to the practice areas • the central team may be able to assist with monitoring compliance and identifying emerging risks and lessons learnt
Paper-based filing system	• where CDD information will be stored so that it can be accessed by fee earners and the MLRO • how monitoring of compliance with CDD obligations will be undertaken • how you will ensure that your restrictions on undertaking work before CDD is completed are enforced
Integrated electronic case management and record-keeping system	• how CDD information will be recorded on your system • which CDD information will be accessible to different parts of the legal practice • how the system will be adapted to ensure that your restrictions on undertaking work before CDD is completed are enforced • how relevant reports can be generated to assist with monitoring compliance

Feature	Risk issues to consider
High use of paralegals and junior staff	• the need to have more formalised procedures • the need to enhance the capacity of the MLRO to answer queries on a more regular basis
High use of qualified and senior staff	• whether you may be able to provide greater flexibility in procedures and give greater discretion to managers/partners

General risk categories for clients, sources of funds and areas of practice

High risk	Medium risk	Low risk
Clients		

• high turnover of clients, or clients who only instruct on single retainers
• clients in or with connection to countries:
   – with poor AML/CTF compliance
   – with poor anti-corruption indicators
   – subject to sanctions
• PEPs from high-risk jurisdictions
• businesses with complicated structures
	• domestic clients from areas with high levels of burglary, theft, fraud, drug dealing or other acquisitive crime
	• domestic PEPs and PEPs from low-risk jurisdictions
	• foreign clients
	• non face-to-face clients or clients otherwise located at a distance from your practice
		• long-standing clients
		• local face-to-face clients
		• FSA regulated businesses
		• local authorities or domestic government departments

Sources of funds		
• businesses which are cash intensive or with income streams which are unclear • high levels of private funding; whether in cash, bank accounts or from third parties with no clear rationale for contributions • public or company funding for private purposes	• legitimate income streams, e.g. wages, government benefits, business profits, etc. • funds from third parties with a clear rationale for contributions • divorce settlements and funds from matters previously handled by other legal practices	• public funding for public projects • loans from a regulated financial institution • funds from matters previously handled by the legal practice, e.g. damages awards, employment termination payments, bequests under a will, etc.

High risk	Medium risk	Low risk
Areas of practice		
• property law, both commercial and residential • corporate law, including company creation, management and acquisition • partnership and trust creation • tax law • insolvency, bankruptcy and receivership • corporate finance • trusts and probate, including acting as an attorney • acting as a Court of Protection deputy	• probate law • regulatory law and professional negligence litigation for individuals and entities in the regulated sector • debt recovery and mortgage repossession • matrimonial and family law • charity law (terrorist financing risks) • intellectual property law • shipping and aviation law (terrorist financing risks) • landlord and tenant law • construction law • environmental, energy and natural resource law • Court of Protection work	• criminal law • professional negligence litigation outside of the regulated sector (such as clinical negligence) • personal injury litigation • other litigation • planning law • children law • mental health and incapacity law • government-funded work • will writing • employment law

Annex 2C
High-risk country checklist

Financial Action Task Force list of countries with unsatisfactory AML controls

For the latest information visit: www.hm-treasury.gov.uk/fin_money_latest_news.htm and www.fatf-gafi.org/topics/high-riskandnon-cooperativejurisdictions

- Bolivia
- Cuba
- Democratic People's Republic of Korea
- Ecuador
- Ethiopia
- Ghana
- Indonesia
- Iran
- Kenya
- Myanmar/Burma
- Nigeria
- Pakistan
- São Tomé and Príncipe
- Sri Lanka
- Syria
- Tanzania
- Thailand
- Turkey
- Vietnam
- Yemen

Sanctions list

For the latest information about the current regimes visit www.hm-treasury.gov.uk/fin_sanctions_index.htm

- Afghanistan
- Al-Qaida
- Belarus
- Democratic People's Republic of Korea (North Korea)
- Democratic Republic of the Congo
- Egypt
- Eritrea
- Federal Republic of Yugoslavia and Serbia
- Iran
- Iraq
- Ivory Coast
- Lebanon

- Liberia
- Libya
- Myanmar/Burma (suspended until 30 April 2013)
- Republic of Guinea
- Republic of Guinea-Bissau
- Somalia
- Sudan
- Syria
- Tunisia
- Zimbabwe

Additional high-risk jurisdictions specific to the legal practice

- [*specify*]

Annex 2D
Risk mitigation form

Key risk areas
List the practice areas which are high risk or involve high-risk clients or jurisdictions:
Outline the legal practice's risk exposure to PEPs and sanctions:

Discharging the MLRO function
Outline the seniority of the MLRO, to whom he or she will report and the relevant support structures in place, including, where relevant, deputies and an AML team:
Outline who will prepare the AML/CTF and sanctions procedures and approve amendments:
Outline who will have discretion to simplify or enhance procedures on a case-by-case basis and how that will be recorded:
Outline how the MLRO will be supported on questions of privilege, negligence and criminal law:
Outline how decisions will be made to exit a client relationship:

Undertaking CDD
List the clients and practice areas which will be subject to CDD requirements:

Outline how CDD will be undertaken: • [centrally/by fee earners/by secretaries] • [electronically/paper based/mixed]
Outline how enhanced due diligence measures will be applied: • for non face-to-face clients   • for PEPs   • for sanctions   • for other high-risk retainers
Outline your policy on accepting cash:
Outline how CDD and other records will be held: • [centrally/on individual files] • [paper based/electronically]
Ensuring compliance
Outline who will be given training:
Outline how compliance will be monitored: • [internal audit team/external audits]

PART 2
Client interface

This section of the toolkit covers how the legal practice will manage its client relationships while meeting its obligations to prevent money laundering, terrorist financing and breaches of the sanctions regime.

3 Client inception

All legal practices undertaking work in the regulated sector must establish and maintain appropriate and risk-sensitive policies and procedures relating to CDD measures. Under MLR 2007, reg.5, CDD measures means:

- identifying the client and verifying his or her identity;
- identifying the beneficial owner, where there is a beneficial owner who is not the client, and taking adequate measures, on a risk-sensitive basis, to verify his or her identity so you are satisfied you know who the beneficial owner is;
- obtaining information on the nature and proposed purpose of the retainer.

Under MLR 2007, reg.7, you must apply CDD measures when you:

- establish a business relationship with a client which you expect to have some element of duration;
- carry out an occasional transaction (i.e. a one-off retainer for a client, the value of which amounts to 15,000 euro or more);
- suspect money laundering or terrorist financing;
- doubt the veracity or adequacy of documents, data or information previously obtained for identification purposes.

The application of those measures is broadly subject to:

- reg.9 (timing of verification);
- reg.13 (simplified due diligence);
- reg.14 (enhanced due diligence);
- reg.17 (reliance).

3.1 Client identification policies and procedures

Your client identification policies and procedures need to be workable, proportionate, sufficiently robust, cost-effective and appropriate for your legal practice and its risk profile. There is no point in having systems which are too difficult or bureaucratic or which are viewed by the legal practice as being not commercial or as preventing business.

Systems for AML/CTF compliance will necessarily interact with and complement other systems including those for client inception and management, case management, financial management, data protection, record keeping, human resources and training. The decisions as to what systems to use or improve will need to involve those responsible for those systems as well as relevant managers/partners to ensure the compatibility of IT systems, especially for record maintenance, case management and, if relevant, e-verification.

Involving the right people at the earliest opportunity will help to ensure any changes are implemented successfully, at a reasonable cost and in a commercial and practical manner.

Once you have considered the above points, you will be able to review and update your procedures to suit your practice.

3.2 Client inception

Good client inception processes are key to the legal practice, capturing the necessary information about the client for regulatory purposes and commercial reasons. Knowing your client helps to build the relationship and capture the client for a range of services in the long term. However, the necessary information must be obtained in a client-friendly way.

You must apply CDD measures to new clients, but the legal practice can determine the extent of those measures on a risk-sensitive basis depending on the type of client, retainer, service or transaction. You must be able to show to the SRA that the extent of those measures is appropriate in view of the risks.

For existing clients, you need to apply CDD measures at other appropriate times on a risk-sensitive basis.

Your procedures will include checking whether a client is a PEP and ensuring that senior management approval is given before a PEP is accepted as a client. Paragraph 4.9.2 of the Law Society's AML practice note provides further guidance about identifying PEPs.

Your procedures will also include the steps you will take to identify beneficial owners and in what circumstances you will require additional information; see para.4.7 of the AML practice note. Whatever procedures you decide to use, it is critical that the ID documents and/or e-verification reports are properly checked to ensure that the information appears accurate and consistent with the information obtained from the client.

3.3 Sanctions

The sanctions regime imposes financial restrictions on persons and entities listed on the HM Treasury's sanctions list so that there are strict liability offences if you receive payment from a person on the sanctions list, deal with his or her economic resources or make payments of any type to those persons. Financial sanctions apply to all transactions including, for example, personal injury work. There is no minimum financial limit.

Legal practices should consider what procedures are required to check whether clients are on the HM Treasury's sanctions list. The procedures need to cover contacting the MLRO if your client is on the sanctions list, as you must suspend the transaction pending advice from the HM Treasury's Asset Freezing Unit, contact the Unit for a licence to deal with the funds and decide if you need to make a report to SOCA.

3.4 Nature of retainer and source of funds

While many may consider that CDD is simply about obtaining identity information, you are also required to understand the nature and the purpose of the retainer. Although, strictly speaking, the source of funds does not have to be established prior to commencing a business relationship, as this is a key area of AML/CTF risk, the earlier this is established, the better placed you will be to assess the risks of that retainer.

Establishing the source of funds is about understanding how the client is funding the retainer, while establishing the source of wealth (which you need to know for a PEP) is about looking at all of the sources of income for an individual, including historical or family funds.

While proof of source of funds or source of wealth is not required, some supporting documentation will help to demonstrate the steps taken to protect the legal practice.

Providing guidance to staff about what documentation to ask for and what questions to ask in the first instance will help them to assess the issues and whether to seek further guidance or consent to proceed from the MLRO.

Where third parties are contributing funds, decisions will need to be made about your procedure, taking into account the risks. You may consider some likely scenarios, for example:

- The money is coming from the wife's parents to buy the couple's first house and you have the parents' ID and details of the amount and source of funds, which are consistent.
- The third party is on benefits and is contributing an amount that is therefore inconsistent with his circumstances. The key is to ask sensible questions and refer the answers to the MLRO for assessment.

3.5 Documenting the process

You need to ensure your process is properly documented so the MLRO knows what to do and the internal audit team knows what to audit. This will include the processes for keeping records of the CDD material, supporting documents and records of the particular transaction in accordance with the legal practice's procedures (see **Chapter 9**).

3.6 Terms of business

Guidance on what to include in your terms of business can be found in the Law Society's client care practice note. You must ensure that you comply with your obligations by including information about obtaining evidence of the client's identity, for example:

- what information will be required from the client;
- if e-verification is used, the data protection position;
- not describing normal postage, telephone calls and charges arising in respect of CDD under MLR 2007 as disbursements (see indicative behaviour (IB) 8.8 of the Code of Conduct).

3.7 Who will decide not to take on a client?

There will be circumstances when the legal practice decides not to take on a client because, for example, it is not satisfied with the CDD. The legal practice needs to determine who will take the decision not to take on a client, and what procedure will be followed.

For most legal practices, the prudent answer will be the MLRO or someone senior in the AML team. It will be very difficult for any manager/partner who has worked hard to win the business to turn down the client, even when the client cannot or will not answer the questions or provide the required information.

Before a client is turned down, the MLRO will review the information and decide what further information is needed, bearing in mind the AML practice note. They may seek guidance from the Law Society's Practice Advice Service.

3.8 Using the toolkit

The client risk assessment and due diligence procedure (**Annex 3A**) will perhaps require the highest level of adaption by the legal practice. The options for conducting due diligence are many and will depend on the other processes for client inception, bearing in mind what types of clients the legal practice has. Essentially the procedure should be adapted to set out clearly who collects what information and when (see the client inception forms at **Annexes 3B** and **3D**).

The client inception verification checklists (**Annexes 3C** and **3E**) should be amended to set out the standard documents which the legal practice is willing to accept to verify identity. The MLRO can vary these documents where appropriate, taking into account the advice in the Law Society's AML practice note.

To determine whether a client may be a PEP, the legal practice may ask clients to complete the form at **Annex 3F** or the legal practice may use e-verification. The MLRO can use the log at **Annex 3G** to monitor PEPs and high-risk clients.

If the legal practice decides to use MLR 2007, reg.17 and rely on or be relied on, **Annex 3H** contains a standard letter.

Employees collecting CDD information will need to be trained on the specific details of the legal practice's processes and requirements. All documents to help employees make decisions on risk assessments, due diligence documents and client-facing forms should be readily accessible, e.g. in the AML manual or on the legal practice's intranet.

Annex 3A
Client risk assessment and due diligence procedure

Purpose

This procedure sets out how [*legal practice name*] will identify and verify the identity of its clients in accordance with its AML/CTF obligations. It also sets out who will be responsible for deciding whether to take on a client.

Application

[*Delete as appropriate:*]

[This procedure applies to all staff.]

[This procedure applies to the MLRO, deputy MLRO [, AML team] and all relevant staff [working in the regulated sector] outlined below:

- managers/partners;
- fee earners;
- paralegals;
- legal secretaries;
- reception staff.]

Failure to comply with this procedure [will/may] result in disciplinary action.

Clients requiring CDD

[*Delete as appropriate:*]

[CDD information will be obtained for all new clients.]

[CDD information will be obtained for all new clients instructing the legal practice in the following areas:

- property;
- corporate and commercial;
- probate/trust;
- tax advice;
- insolvency;
- acting as an attorney or Court of Protection deputy;
- [*specify any other areas*].]

[CDD information will be obtained for all new clients other than those instructing the legal practice in the following areas:

- [*specify any other areas – must be non-regulated work*].]

The CDD information and risk assessment must be reviewed for all existing clients when they instruct [*legal practice name*] on a new retainer. The risk assessment must be updated for the new retainer and consideration given as to whether CDD information needs to be updated.

Information required

For relevant clients, [*legal practice name*] requires information:

- identifying the client in accordance with the relevant client verification checklist;
- identifying the beneficial owners, where required, in accordance with the relevant client verification checklist;
- on the nature and purpose of the retainer;
- on the source of funds to be used in the retainer, where relevant.

[*Legal practice name*] will undertake verification of identity information [predominantly through provision of source documents/predominantly through e-verification/through provision of source documents, e-verification and other sources].

[Completing the client inception form/Entering details into the case management system]

Prior to the first interview with the client (in person or by telephone) the [secretary/fee earner/AML team], will obtain the client's name, date of birth (where relevant), address and phone number.

The [fee earner/secretary] is responsible for [completing the client inception form/entering details into the case management system]. They will:

- confirm the identity details with the client;
- complete the retainer details section after taking instructions; and
- complete the risk assessment section of the client inception form with reference to the risk identification matrix and the high-risk countries checklist for [*legal practice name*].

The fee earner or AML team will assess the appropriate standard of due diligence required and ensure that the appropriate verification, as outlined in the relevant verification checklist, is undertaken and [recorded in the document section of the client inception form/entered into the case management system].

Where there is a high risk rating for the area of law, client type, or jurisdiction, or a reason to conduct enhanced due diligence, the fee earner will refer the matter to the [AML team/deputy MLRO/MLRO] for advice on the appropriate due diligence measures to take.

Where a client is not seen face-to-face, the due diligence documents must be certified by [a solicitor/a notary/an accountant/a post office/a doctor/*other*] or undertake e-verification and the first payment of fees must come from an account with a financial institution which is held in the client's name.

Obtaining verification information

[*Delete as appropriate:*]

[Prior to the first interview, e-verification checks will be undertaken for all [clients/ private clients/private clients and companies] by the [secretary/fee earner/AML team] to verify identity and check against sanctions lists and for PEPs.]

[Private clients will be asked to bring standard due diligence documents to the first interview in accordance with the client verification checklist. If further documents are required following the risk assessment, the [fee earner/secretary/AML team] is responsible for obtaining these from the client.]

[The fee earner will ask all [foreign] private clients to complete the PEP checklist during their first interview.]

[The [fee earner/secretary/AML team] will conduct a sanctions list check [via the HM Treasury website/using an e-verification provider] where the client, retainer or source of funds is related to a sanctioned jurisdiction/regime.]

[The [fee earner/secretary/AML team] will ask [private clients/entity and legal arrangement clients/all clients] by [email/letter] to provide the required due diligence documents after the risk assessment has been completed.]

[The [fee earner/AML team] will undertake electronic checks and liaise with the client or other relevant individuals to obtain information on and verification of beneficial ownership as set out in the relevant verification checklist.]

[Copies of due diligence documents will be taken by the [reception staff/secretary/ fee earner]. Where a due diligence document includes photographic identification, the [reception staff/secretary/fee earner] will assess the document and certify that it is a true likeness. If they are unable to provide this certification, they should raise the matter with the MLRO.]

Where a client appears to be a PEP or on a sanctions list, guidance must be sought from the [MLRO/deputy MLRO/AML team] before any further action is taken.

If the client appears to be on a sanctions list, the MLRO will decide what further action is required.

If, following investigation, it is decided that the potential client is a PEP, the MLRO must give senior management approval before the client can be accepted. Such clients will then be subject to ongoing review by the MLRO [and the fee earner].

Timing of verification of identity

Identity information should be verified within [*specify time frame*] of the [first interview/receipt of the client care letter] for private clients and within [*specify time frame, e.g. one week*] for entities and legal arrangements.

If the fee earner is aware that there will be delays in obtaining verification evidence, the reason for the delay must be discussed with the [MLRO/AML team] and a timescale agreed.

[*Delete as appropriate:*]

[A file number will not be issued, work cannot be commenced and time cannot be recorded on a file until the client due diligence form has been completed.]

[Work can only be undertaken on a file to the value of £[*X*] before the client due diligence form has been completed. Funds cannot be received or paid out until the client due diligence form has been completed.]

[*Specify any other restrictions or exemptions.*]

If verification is not completed within [*specify time frame, e.g. one month*], the [MLRO/AML team] will close the file for time recording.

Reliance

[*Delete as appropriate:*]

[[*Legal practice name*] will not agree to be relied upon for due diligence.]

[[*Legal practice name*] will not rely upon others for due diligence.]

[[*Legal practice name*] will permit reliance in the following circumstances:

- [A barrister we are instructing may rely on [*legal practice name*] for due diligence regarding our client.]
- [We may ask to rely upon an accountant registered with a professional body in England and Wales who referred a client to [*legal practice name*].]
- [*Specify other circumstances*].]

All reliance requests must be approved by the [MLRO/deputy MLRO/AML team].

All reliance requests must be made or confirmed using the letter of introduction for reliance.

Where reliance is permitted, this should be noted in the documentation section of the client inception form. All other parts of the client inception form must be completed.

Source of funds

The fee earner must obtain information about the source of funds on all retainers and monitor whether monies are coming from expected and credible sources.

The fee earner must consider the risk identification matrix and take the following action:

- For a low-risk source of funds, the fee earner should record the proposed source of funds and check that the funds come from that source.
- For a medium-risk source of funds, the fee earners should record the proposed source of funds, ask the client for evidence to verify this source and check that the funds come from that source.
- For a high-risk source of funds, the fee earner should consult with the [MLRO/ deputy MLRO/AML team] as to the appropriate documentation required to verify the source.
- For a PEP, the fee earner must ask about the source of funds for the retainer and understand the PEP's general source of wealth. Fee earners should consult with the [MLRO/deputy MLRO/AML team] about how to verify this information.

The fee earner must advise the MLRO and the accounts team if there are large or unusual levels of funding involved in a retainer or if they are coming from unusual or high-risk sources or jurisdictions.

If a payment is being made by a third party, the fee earner must ask why the third party is helping with funding, obtain the name of the third party [and evidence of identity] and require that the funds are provided from an account in the third party's name.

Record-keeping

The [fee earner/MLRO/AML team] is responsible for ensuring that records are kept of due diligence measures undertaken and all supporting documents.

[*Delete as appropriate:*]

[Completed client inception forms and supporting documents are to be retained in hard copy [on the client file/centrally].]

[Completed client inception forms and supporting documents are to be scanned and held electronically.]

[The client inception details are to be completed in the case management system and scanned supporting documents attached.]

MLRO discretion

The MLRO retains the discretion to apply different procedures to an individual case or class of cases within the scope permitted by the risk-based approach under the Money Laundering Regulations 2007.

When this discretion is exercised, the MLRO must:

- note this [on the client inception form/in the case management system] together with the reasons for exercising the discretion;
- consider whether this procedure needs to be amended or updated.

Related policy

Anti-money laundering, counter-terrorist financing and sanctions compliance policy

Glossary

AML	anti-money laundering
CDD	client due diligence
CTF	counter-terrorist financing
MLRO	money laundering reporting officer, also known as a nominated officer
PEP	politically exposed person

Date of effect/date of review

This procedure shall come into effect on [date]. This procedure shall be reviewed annually.

Annex 3B
Private client inception form

Identity details
Client name:
Date of birth:
Nationality:
Address:
Postcode:
Telephone number:
Email address:
Occupation:
Are they acting on behalf of another person? Y/N

Retainer details
Matter or nature and purpose of instructions:
Source of funds and amount:
Does this make sense in terms of the legal practice and the risk profile of the client? Y/N Explain why:

Risk assessment	
Area of law:	Risk rating:
Client type:	Risk rating:
Jurisdiction:	Risk rating:
Is simplified due diligence permitted? Y/N Explain why:	
Is enhanced due diligence required? Y/N If yes, select reason: ☐ PEP ☐ Non face-to-face ☐ Other:	

CDD standard to be applied:		
☐ Simplified	☐ Standard	☐ Enhanced
Documentation		
Client verified electronically: Y/N		
Sanctions list checked: Y/N		
Original documents of identity seen: Y/N		
Evidence of identity attached: Y/N		
Is any photograph a good likeness? Y/N		
What enhanced measures were taken (if required)?		

Person completing CDD	Management sign-off (if required)
Signed:	Signed:
Name:	Name:
Position:	Position:
Date:	Date:

Annex 3C
Private client verification checklist

For standard due diligence you are required to obtain the following information to verify the identity of a private client.

Either:

- one document in category A or B which verifies name and current address OR name and date of birth;
- one document in category B which verifies name and one document in category C which verifies name and address or date of birth, which is less than three months old.

If the client is unable to produce any documents on the lists, contact the MLRO for further guidance.

Category A	Category B	Category C
• e-verification report	• UK/EU drivers licence • UK passport • Foreign passport or identity card • Birth certificate	• Firearms certificate • State pensions/benefits book or notification letter • Council tax bill • Bank/building society/ mortgage statement • Local council/housing association rent card or tenancy agreement • HMRC tax notification

Other considerations

For specific categories of clients you should use the following verification methods:

Category of client	Document required
Client in care home	Letter from the manager
Refugee	Home Office letter or travel document
[Specify other categories]	

Acting for others

If the client is acting on behalf of another person you should also obtain the name, address and date of birth of the person on whose behalf he or she is acting and the following documents to verify his or her authority to act on that person's behalf:

Category of client	Document required
Professional client acting in his or her professional capacity	Print out of his or her listing on the directory held by the relevant regulatory body
Person exercising a power of attorney or acting as a Court of Protection deputy	Power of attorney document or court order appointing the deputy
Agent, broker, etc.	Letter of appointment

Annex 3D
Entity or legal arrangement client inception form

Identity details
Client name:
Type of entity: ☐ Company ☐ Partnership ☐ Trust ☐ Government ☐ Other
Nature of business:
Company number or equivalent:
Registered address:
Trading address if different to above:
Telephone number:
Country of incorporation or constitution:

Contact details
Name of main contact and position:
Direct telephone number:
Direct email address:

Retainer details
Matter or nature and purpose of instructions:
Source of funds and amount:
Does this make sense in terms of the legal practice and the risk profile of the client? Y/N   Explain why:

Risk assessment	
Area of law:	Risk rating:
Client type:	Risk rating:
Jurisdiction:	Risk rating:
Is simplified due diligence permitted? Y/N Explain why:	

CDD standard to be applied:		
☐ Simplified	☐ Standard	☐ Enhanced

Documentation
Client verified electronically? Y/N
Sanctions list checked? Y/N
Evidence of identity for entity or arrangement attached? Y/N
Evidence of beneficial owners attached? Y/N
What enhanced measures were taken (if required)?

Person completing CDD	**Management sign-off (if required)**
Signed:	Signed:
Name:	Name:
Position:	Position:
Date:	Date:

Annex 3E
Entity or legal arrangement client verification checklist

You should obtain the relevant details and documents below to verify the identity of an entity or legal arrangement.

If you are unsure as to the documents you should obtain, are having difficulty obtaining any documents, or if a client has a higher risk rating for an area of law or a jurisdiction, contact the MLRO for advice on the specific evidence required.

Entity or arrangement type	Evidence of identity	Evidence of beneficial ownership	
Professional regulated partnership	Copy of the partnership's listing, including address in the professional body directory	Standard	Name of any partner who has more than 25% of the capital or profits of the partnership or more than 25% of the voting rights or any other person with control over the partnership
		Higher risk rating for identity	Copy of passport or e-verification of partners listed above
Partnership			
• Publicly well known	Evidence of: • name • registered address and trading address • nature of business	Name of any partner who has more than 25% of the capital or profits of the partnership or more than 25% of the voting rights or any other person with control over the partnership	
• Small	Evidence of identity for two partners (including the partner instructing you) as for private clients	In addition to the two partners, the name of any partner who has more than 25% of the capital or profits of the partnership or more than 25% of the voting rights or any other person with control over the partnership. If higher risk rating for identity, verify his or her details	
• Large	Evidence as per a private company (see below)	Name of any partner who has more than 25% of the capital or profits of the partnership or more than 25% of the voting rights or any other person with control over the partnership. If higher risk rating for identity, verify his or her details	

Entity or arrangement type	Evidence of identity	Evidence of beneficial ownership	
Company listed on the following exchanges: • London Stock Exchange • [*specify other*]	Simplified due diligence applies; obtain one of the following: • copy of the dated page of the website of the relevant stock exchange showing the listing • copy of the listing in a reputable daily newspaper • copy of the listing from the online registry • e-verification report	Not required	
Wholly owned and consolidated subsidiary of listed company (as above)	Simplified due diligence applies; obtain the following: • identity information for the parent company • evidence of the parent/ entity relationship	Not required	
Private company or company listed on other exchanges	Obtain one of the following: • company listing on online registry • e-verification report • certificate of incorporation Ensure the document shows: • name of company • registered and business address(es) • names of two directors	Standard	Name of any individual who owns more than 25% of voting rights or otherwise exercises control over the management of the company
		Higher risk rating for identiy	Verify the above information by obtaining a copy of one of the following: • written advice from the company's legal team • listing on the online company registry • e-verification report

Entity or arrangement type	Evidence of identity	Evidence of beneficial ownership	
Trust	• If the trust is a company, obtain the documents for a company • If the trust is an individual, obtain the documents for a private client • If you are acting for more than one trustee, verify the identity of at least two of the trustees	Standard	• Names of trustees • Name of any individual with a specified interest of at least 25% in trust capital or who controls the trust • Describe the class of persons in whose main interest the trust operates Note: if acting for the executors of a deceased's estate, only the names of the executors are relevant
		Higher risk rating for identity	As above, but verify the names by obtaining one of the following: • written assurances from the trustees • written assurances from other regulated individuals • an e-verification check on the identified individuals
UK or EEA Public Authority (including local government)	Simplified due diligence applies in the UK and may apply to an EEA public authority	Not applicable	
Other public body	Evidence of: • name • registered address and trading address • nature of business • type of public body	Names of individuals instructing the legal practice and details of their authority to instruct you	

Entity or arrangement type	Evidence of identity	Evidence of beneficial ownership	
Charity	• If the charity is registered, obtain a copy of its listing on the charities register • If the charity is not registered, consider the business structure of the charity and verify in accordance with the business structure	As per the business structure of the charity	
Club or association	Copy of one of the following: • articles of association or constitution • statement from a financial institution • recent audited accounts • listing in local or national telephone directory Ensure the document shows: • full name of the association • any registered address • names of all office holders	Standard	• Names of any individuals who benefit from or control at least 25% of the property of the association • Describe the class of persons in whose main interest the club or association is operated
		Higher risk rating for identity	As above, but verify the names by obtaining one of the following: • written assurances from the client • written assurances from other regulated individuals • copy of the constitution or membership rules
Pension fund			
• Employer pension fund	Simplified due diligence applies; obtain a copy of either: • a page showing the name of the scheme from the most recent definitive deed • a consolidating deed for the scheme, plus any amending deed subsequent to that date	Not applicable	
• Other pension fund	As per the business structure of the fund	As per the business structure of the fund	

Annex 3F
Client PEP form

UK regulations require [*legal practice name*] to review more closely retainers with clients who are known as politically exposed persons (PEPs).

To help us to meet these obligations, please complete the form below and return it with your signed client care letter.

Failure to complete this form may result in delays or mean that we cannot act for you.

Please tick any category which applies to you:				
Role	I hold one of these roles	I am acting on behalf of someone who holds one of these roles in this case	A family member[1] holds one of these roles	I am in business[2] with someone who holds one of these roles
Member of the Royal Family	☐	☐	☐	☐
President or Prime Minister	☐	☐	☐	☐
Member of Parliament	☐	☐	☐	☐
Holder of a senior appointment with an international organisation	☐	☐	☐	☐
Ambassador	☐	☐	☐	☐
Chargé d'affaires	☐	☐	☐	☐
Judge (in a court of appeal or higher court)	☐	☐	☐	☐
Member of the court of auditors	☐	☐	☐	☐
Member of the board of the central bank	☐	☐	☐	☐
Member of the board of management of a state owned enterprise	☐	☐	☐	☐

Holder of the following rank (or equivalent) in the military: • Field Marshal • General • Marshal • Air Chief Marshal • Admiral	☐	☐	☐	☐
If you have ticked any of the above, please provide details of your role or your relationship with the person in that role:				
1. 'A family member' means your spouse, partner, parent, child or child's spouse or partner. 2. 'In business with' means joint ownership of a company, partnership or association.				

Signed:
Name:
Date:

Annex 3G

MLRO log of PEP and high-risk clients

Name	Occupation	Nationality	Reason for potential PEP	Country of residence	Political connections	Source of wealth and funds/ amounts	Key issues considered	Senior manage- ment approval	Ongoing monitoring: review date

Annex 3H
Letter of introduction for reliance

Date:

To: [*legal practice name*]

Dear Sirs,

Re: [*name of introduced person*] of [*address of introduced person*]

I confirm that we have carried out customer due diligence measures under the Money Laundering Regulations 2007 ('the Regulations') and have verified the identity of:

Full name of client:

Address:

Date of birth:

[*Delete as appropriate:*]

[In so doing we concluded that there is no beneficial owner.]

[In so doing we concluded that there [is/are] the following beneficial owner[s], and we have taken adequate measures on a risk-sensitive basis to verify their identity:

Full name of beneficial owner:

Address:

Date of birth:]

We consent to you relying upon our due diligence, for the purposes of regulation 17 of the Regulations. We confirm that we are an organisation falling within regulation 17(2) of the Regulations (see notes). We acknowledge that, in accordance with regulation 19, if you so request, we will as soon as practicable:

(a) make available to you any information about the client (and any beneficial owner) which we obtained when applying customer due diligence measures; and

(b) forward to you copies of any identification and verification data and other relevant documents on the identity of the client (and any beneficial owner) which we obtained when applying those measures.

Full name of introducer:

FSA registration number:

Other regulator number:

Signed:

Name and position:

Notes

Regulation 17(2) provides that such organisations are:

(a) a credit or financial institution which is an authorised person;
(aa) a consumer credit financial institution;
(b) a relevant person who is –

    (i) an auditor, insolvency practitioner, external accountant, tax adviser or independent legal professional; and
    (ii) supervised for the purposes of these Regulations by one of the bodies listed in Schedule 3;

(c) a person who carries on business in another EEA state who is –

    (i) a credit or financial institution, auditor, insolvency practitioner, external accountant, tax adviser or independent legal professional;
    (ii) subject to mandatory professional registration recognised by law; and
    (iii) supervised for compliance with the requirements laid down in the money laundering directive in accordance with section 2 of Chapter V of that directive; or

(d) a person who carries on business in a non-EEA state who is –

    (i) a credit or financial institution (or equivalent institution), auditor, insolvency practitioner, external accountant, tax adviser or independent legal professional;
    (ii) subject to mandatory professional registration recognised by law;
    (iii) subject to requirements equivalent to those laid down in the money laundering directive; and
    (iv) supervised for compliance with those requirements in a manner equivalent to section 2 of Chapter V of the money laundering directive.

The EEA states are the members of the EU, namely Austria, Belgium, Bulgaria, Cyprus, the Czech Republic, Denmark, Estonia, Finland, France, Germany, Greece, Hungary, Ireland, Italy, Latvia, Lithuania, Luxembourg, Malta, the Netherlands, Poland, Portugal, Romania, Slovakia, Slovenia, Spain, Sweden and the UK, plus Liechtenstein, Iceland and Norway.

The following non-EEA states may be considered as having equivalent anti-money laundering and counter-terrorist financing systems for the purposes of regulation 17: Australia, Brazil, Canada, Hong Kong, India, Japan, South Korea, Mexico, Singapore, Switzerland, South Africa and the USA.

Source: European Commission, 26 June 2012, **http://ec.europa.eu/internal_market/ company/financial-crime/index_en.htm**

4 Due diligence during the retainer

4.1 Keeping records up to date

CDD information must be kept up to date under MLR 2007, reg.8. This does not mean that full verification is required every time a client instructs you on another retainer. However it is important that fee earners remember to stay alert to changes in identity information and in the client's risk levels, which may require additional due diligence.

4.2 Ongoing monitoring

Under MLR 2007, reg.8, legal practices must also conduct ongoing monitoring of a business relationship where the work is in the regulated sector.

Ongoing monitoring means keeping a client and the retainer under review to ensure that the transactions are consistent with your knowledge of the client, his or her business and the risk profile. This means the scrutiny of transactions undertaken during the course of the relationship, including continued monitoring of the source of funds.

Ensuring that staff understand the importance of due diligence during the retainer is arguably the most important element of MLR 2007. Staff must ask questions if they are unsure or concerned about a client or a retainer. Failure to realise there is a potential concern could lead to allegations of a failure to report or of a breach of reg.8. Such allegations would affect the individual as well as the legal practice.

You must review your areas of risk and decide what systems and procedures will work best for your legal practice. Whatever systems are in place, your staff must have easy access to the MLRO or AML team, who must be approachable, responsive, knowledgeable, commercial and trusted by your staff.

4.3 Issues for staff to consider

You will need to provide guidance on what issues staff must consider and what warning signs to look for. Explaining the importance of 'knowing your client' to staff is critical because they can then assess whether the transactions, etc. are consistent with the client's risk profile.

'Knowing your client' is broader than identifying and verifying the client's identity. It is about gathering information during the retainer and being able to assess whether the information you have gained 'makes sense' and is consistent. Most fee earners will be obtaining this information in any event, but they may not appreciate its value in terms of AML protection.

4.4 Warning signs

As part of the training, you will need to highlight the warning signs relevant to the risk profile of your legal practice. Chapter 11 of the Law Society's AML practice note provides examples of warning signs.

4.5 Discussions with the MLRO

Helping staff to identify when to seek guidance is critical for the protection of the legal practice and its staff. The emphasis should always be on seeking guidance because the risk is that, given the complexity of the law, making a decision could result in criminal offences, regulatory offences or disciplinary sanctions.

The MLRO must be accessible and staff must know how to contact him or her. The MLRO will want to record AML queries so that common themes and trends can be identified (see the MLRO query log at **Annex 4B**). This information will help you to identify training needs within particular teams and may also result in drafting new or amending existing procedures so that your systems are more robust and effective.

The MLRO will need to assess the information and give appropriate guidance on individual matters.

4.6 Using the toolkit

Essentially most of the ongoing monitoring will be done by fee earners. The ongoing monitoring procedure (**Annex 4A**) will set out their obligations and will need to be available to all staff, preferably in the AML manual or on the intranet.

Where fee earners ask questions about warning signs, they should make a note of the question asked, the answer provided and any supporting documents obtained. While care should be taken not to write on the file 'I suspect this person is a money launderer', you may wish to advise fee earners to make a note on the file that they have 'discussed regulatory matters' if they have engaged in extended consultation on a matter with the MLRO.

It is also important, particularly where there are potential reporting issues or POCA concerns, that the fee earner also keeps the notes and emails on a separate file. Each team should hold a separate POCA file because of the risks of keeping such information on the client file, should the file be called for by the police or the client.

The MLRO may wish to keep records (e.g. emails or notes of conversations) for more detailed queries in a folder or separate files. Internal reports and MLRO decisions should also be recorded and maintained in the event of any further enquiries.

Annex 4A

Ongoing monitoring procedure

Purpose

[*Legal practice name*] is committed to compliance with its AML/CTF obligations, in order to mitigate the risks of its services being used by money launderers or terrorist financers.

This procedure sets out how [*legal practice name*] will ensure that due diligence measures are undertaken throughout the life of a retainer and general queries are raised with the [MLRO/deputy MLRO/AML team].

Application

[*Delete as appropriate:*]

[This procedure applies to all staff.]

[This procedure applies to the MLRO, deputy MLRO, AML team and all managers/ partners, fee earners and paralegals.]

Keeping due diligence information up to date

For all retainers where CDD is required, the information to verify the client's identity will be updated where there is:

- a change in identity details or beneficial ownership details;
- a gap in retainers of [*specify time frame, e.g. three years or more*];
- a change in the risk profile of the client requiring enhanced due diligence;
- [*specify other circumstances*].

These changes may occur between retainers or during a retainer.

[*Delete as appropriate:*]

[It is the responsibility of the fee earner to update the verification information.]

[It is the responsibility of the fee earner to notify the [MLRO/deputy MLRO/AML team] of changes requiring an update of the verification information.]

Steps must be taken to update the information within [*specify time frame, e.g. one week*] of the fee earner becoming aware of the change.

If the verification information cannot be updated within [*specify time frame, e.g. one month*] of the fee earner becoming aware of the change, the matter must be referred to the [MLRO/deputy MLRO] for a decision on whether [*legal practice name*] can continue to act for the client.

Ongoing monitoring of a retainer

During all retainers, fee earners must stay alert to:

- warning signs of money laundering or terrorist financing;
- information which suggests that the CDD material previously provided is false or otherwise incorrect;
- whether the developments in the retainer are consistent with the risk profile and nature of the business of the client;
- material changes to the client, nature of the retainer or source or destination of funds which will alter the risk assessment conducted at the outset of the retainer.

[*Delete as appropriate:*]

[Where a fee earner notices any of these factors in a retainer, he or she must raise them with [his or her supervisor/the AML team/the deputy MLRO/the MLRO] within [*specify time frame, e.g. 24 hours*].]

Where the [supervisor/AML team/deputy MLRO/MLRO] recommends that further enquiries are made of the client, the fee earner should make those enquiries and make a note of both the enquiry and the response provided.

In discussion with the [supervisor/AML team/deputy MLRO/MLRO], the fee earner must consider whether his or her concerns are now adequately addressed, whether further information is required or whether he or she has a suspicion of money laundering requiring an internal report.

Where matters are raised with the [supervisor/AML team/deputy MLRO/MLRO], the fee earner must provide his or her details and details of the client, matter number, type of retainer and nature of query.

The [supervisor/AML team/deputy MLRO/MLRO] must record those details on the attached form and provide appropriate guidance, including what advice was provided and when and how it was provided.

Related policy

Anti-money laundering, counter-terrorist financing and sanctions compliance policy

Glossary

AML   anti-money laundering

CDD   client due diligence

CTF   counter-terrorist financing

MLRO   money laundering reporting officer, also known as a nominated officer

Date of effect/date of review

This procedure shall come into effect on [*date*]. This procedure shall be reviewed annually.

Annex 4B

MLRO query log

Date and time	Fee earner/ department	Matter/file no. and client name	Query	Advice provided	Method of providing advice, date and time	Follow-up action/trends

5 Managing risks around source of funds

Legal practices should already have systems and procedures in place to minimise the risk of client accounts being used for money laundering or terrorist financing. In conjunction with the compliance officer for finance and administration (COFA), the MLRO should ensure that these systems and procedures are regularly reviewed and updated. The COFA will ensure compliance with the SRA Accounts Rules 2011, which set out the basic requirements for handling client monies, through systems for reporting, recording and remedying breaches.

The AML aspects of the accounting systems are likely to include:

- not acting as a bank;
- having a cash policy;
- systems for receipt of monies;
- reviewing sources of funds; and
- identifying transactions of concern.

5.1 Underlying transactions

Under rule 14.5 of the SRA Accounts Rules 2011, you must not provide banking facilities through a client account; and payments into, and transfers or withdrawals from, a client account must relate to an underlying transaction or to a service forming part of your normal regulated activities.

Any guidance to staff in relation to this area should include a reminder that the 'accepting deposits' exemption in art.7 of the Financial Services and Markets Act 2000 (Regulated Activities) Order 2001, SI 2001/544 is likely to be lost if a deposit is taken in circumstances which do not form part of the practice. Failure to comply with this provision can result in disciplinary action for employees. Everyone in the legal practice must be clear that the legal practice cannot act as a bank.

5.2 Cash policy

Legal practices are advised to have a policy on handling cash, as cash can be a warning sign of money laundering. The issues to consider are:

- what is the limit?
- who will give approval in exceptional circumstances?
- what audit trail will you have?

- how will you advise staff, including reception and accounts staff?
- including a clause about the policy in your terms of business.

A cash policy enables the legal practice to review the amount, the transaction and the client and assess the money laundering risks. Clients may try to deposit cash directly into your client account with your bank, so it is prudent to have a procedure for such circumstances.

5.3 Receipt of monies

A legal practice's accounting systems should ensure that monies received from clients are properly recorded and allocated to clients. The accounts team need to be able to identify the client to whom the money relates, where the money has come from (e.g. which bank account and the account holder's name), which jurisdiction the money emanated from and whether it is the right amount.

It will be prudent to give clear instructions to the client about what information to provide about the source of the money and payment details. Good liaison between the fee earners and the accounts team should mean that if there are concerns, they can be identified quickly and guidance sought from the MLRO.

In reviewing your systems, you are likely to consider, for example, the risks posed by monies coming from a company account instead of a personal account (i.e. is this proper use of company assets?), monies being received without payment details so that the source is difficult to identify, monies coming from a third party or unexpected source or more money being received than expected.

Client account cheques are useful to money launderers because it is assumed that the funds have been thoroughly vetted when received. Being asked to return money because too much has been sent, it has been sent by mistake or the transaction is abortive can be money laundering. Good, robust accounting systems and ensuring fee earners ask the right questions should minimise those risks.

5.4 Source of funds

The accounting procedures should enable concerns about the source of funds to be identified and discussed with the MLRO. If monies are coming from a high value dealer or a money services business, is the business registered with HMRC under MLR 2007? If the client is a cash business or self-employed, is it, he or she registered with HMRC? If not, it is likely that you need to review the risks of tax evasion.

5.5 Identifying transactions of concern

As a result of their AML training, staff should identify transactions of concern and raise those concerns with the MLRO. The accounts team may see patterns or transactions not seen by fee earners, so they need different training to identify concerns. The escalation process for such transactions needs to be included in the procedure.

A legal practice that wishes to hold monies as stakeholder or on escrow should consider what safeguards to put in place, for example, how it will determine the source of funds, the identity of those sending money, the reason for the request, how long the practice will hold the money, who will be entitled to the interest and under what circumstances the money will be repaid and how. See para.11.5.2 of the Law Society's AML practice note.

5.6 Sanctions

The sanctions regime applies to payments received or made by the legal practice. The accounts team should check all payment requests against the high-risk country checklist (see **Annex 2C**) and alert the MLRO to any proposed payments to possible sanctioned jurisdictions/regimes or clients.

5.7 Using the toolkit

Ensuring that the accounts team understand their obligations and how to protect the legal practice will be critical. They need relevant training and sufficient support if they raise concerns. Fee earners and accounts staff need easy access to the procedure for accepting cash and monitoring accounts (**Annex 5A**).

Annex 5A
Procedure for accepting cash and monitoring accounts

Purpose

[*Legal practice name*] is committed to compliance with its AML/CTF obligations, in order to mitigate the risks of its services being used by money launderers or terrorist financers.

This procedure sets out how [*legal practice name*] will ensure that the risk of [*legal practice name*]'s bank accounts being used by money launderers or terrorist financers is minimised.

Application

This procedure applies to all staff in [*legal practice name*] and sets out the requirements for dealing with client monies. Failure to comply with this procedure [will/may] result in disciplinary action.

Accounts staff must exercise additional care and seek further information from employees and managers/partners if any aspect of a transaction causes concern, does not appear to be as expected or is unusual.

Use of client account

The client account must not be used to provide banking services; there must be an underlying legal transaction, e.g. acting as an attorney or trustee. Guidance as to whether there is an underlying legal transaction must be sought from the [MLRO/ AML team].

[*Legal practice name*]'s procedures for the receipt of monies into the client account are set out in its accounting procedures and policy. [*Legal practice name*] will require information about the source of funds.

Banking details must only be disclosed to clients when funds are expected. All clients must provide payment details including their name, reference, [*further details, e.g. bank statement or letter showing debited funds and the account holder's name and account number or other evidence*].

Cash

[*Legal practice name*] does not accept cash over [*specify limit*] [except in exceptional circumstances, when it must be approved by the MLRO].

If clients bring in cash of [*specify limit*] or less to reception, the receptionist must immediately contact the accounts team so the monies can be counted and a valid receipt given.

If clients bring in cash over [*specify limit*] to reception, the receptionist must immediately contact the fee earner.

The fee earner must advise the client that the cash cannot be accepted, reminding him or her of the provision in the terms of business.

If there are exceptional reasons as to why the fee earner believes the cash should be accepted, the MLRO must be contacted.

If the MLRO agrees the cash can be accepted, the fee earner must contact the accounts team who must count the cash and give a valid receipt to the client.

When the cash is being banked, [*legal practice name*] will provide appropriate security for the relevant member of staff. If the cash is received after banking hours, it must be placed in the safe overnight and banked promptly the next day.

If the accounts team is advised that a client has brought in cash, they must immediately contact the fee earner and remind him or her of [*legal practice name*]'s policy [and advise the fee earner that the cash can only be accepted with the MLRO's consent].

If the accounts team is advised by the bank that cash has been deposited directly into [*legal practice name*]'s bank account, they must obtain full details of the client and an explanation as to why this has happened. Guidance must then be sought from the [MLRO/AML team] as to what steps to take.

Holding funds on escrow

If you are asked to hold funds on escrow, you must seek guidance from the [MLRO/ AML team].

Sanctions

The accounts team must check all payment requests against the high-risk country checklist and alert the MLRO immediately to any proposed payments to possible sanctioned jurisdictions/regimes or clients.

Identifying transactions of concern

Accounts staff and those in fee-earning teams must review whether there are patterns of client money activity which cause concern and raise those concerns with the [MLRO/AML team].

All staff must be aware of the warning signs for money laundering and raise any concerns with the [MLRO/AML team].

Queries about monies or source of funds

Accounts staff must raise any concerns or queries about a transaction, source of funds or financial issue with the [MLRO/AML team], providing details of the client, matter number, type of retainer and nature of query.

The [MLRO/AML team] will record those details on the MLRO query log and provide appropriate guidance, recording what advice was provided and when and how it was provided.

Related policy

Anti-money laundering, counter-terrorist financing and sanctions compliance policy

Glossary

AML	anti-money laundering
consent	permission to proceed with a retainer even though there is a suspicion of money laundering
CTF	counter-terrorist financing
MLRO	money laundering reporting officer, also known as a nominated officer

Date of effect/date of review

This procedure shall come into effect on [*date*]. This procedure shall be reviewed annually.

6 Making reports

Legal practices have reporting obligations under both MLR 2007 and POCA 2002, so the policies and procedures will need to cover all the regulatory obligations.

Under MLR 2007, reg.20, a legal practice must establish and maintain appropriate and risk-sensitive policies and procedures relating to reporting, which will set out:

- what employees and managers/partners must do if they have concerns about a client, retainer or transaction;
- the procedure that the MLRO must then follow to protect the legal practice.

As a result of the training provided by the legal practice, employees and managers/partners will recognise the circumstances in which they need to make reports under MLR 2007 and POCA 2002 to the MLRO.

6.1 Internal reports

The legal practice will need to decide the procedure for making internal reports and whether a report should only be made after a request for guidance has been considered. The procedure should make it clear that fee earners must report to the MLRO and not report direct to SOCA.

The procedure needs to ensure the MLRO receives all the information necessary to make a decision as to whether he or she has knowledge or suspicion of, or reasonable grounds to know or suspect, money laundering or terrorist financing.

The MLRO must be available to employees and managers/partners, who will need support and guidance in dealing with potentially difficult situations and clients. The MLRO may need to strike a balance between being sympathetic, being commercial and protecting the legal practice and its employees.

6.2 External reports

The MLRO is responsible for making a SAR to SOCA as soon as practicable after he or she has formed a reportable suspicion or acquired reportable knowledge of terrorist financing or money laundering (subject to privilege considerations).

Before making the decision whether to report and to whom, the MLRO will consider the legislation and apply it to the circumstances of the particular matter. The flow charts at Annex 6D will help in assessing whether to report. For further information see chapters 5 and 7 of the Law Society's AML practice note.

Having considered the law, the MLRO will consider chapter 6 of the AML practice note and whether the information is privileged or received in privileged circumstances or whether the crime/fraud exception applies.

In addition, the MLRO should consider whether it is ethical to seek consent and continue to act or whether you should terminate the retainer or alternatively report but withdraw from acting. Any decision to terminate the retainer will be taken in conjunction with the COLP, bearing in mind the ethical issues considered in **Chapter 7**.

In making a report to SOCA and obtaining consent (permission to proceed with a retainer even though there is a suspicion of money laundering), the legal practice/MLRO is only protected from committing an offence under the anti-money laundering regime. The legal practice is not protected from civil liability and there may be occasions where a report is made but the legal practice decides that it is not ethically appropriate to continue acting. Considerable care is needed in this area. Chapter 10 of the AML practice note provides assistance, but if you believe you may have acted as a constructive trustee, you should seek legal advice.

6.3 Practicalities

The report will be in the form of either a SAR or a limited intelligence value report (LIVR). As explained in para.8.3.4 of the Law Society's AML practice note, the former will be the norm.

Legal practices should use SOCA's SAR Online if they have computer and internet access. Links to information about how to register and what to include in a report are found at paras.8.3.5 and 8.3.6 of the AML practice note.

The report should set out clearly the reason for the suspicion, details of the offence, who is involved, whether you are seeking consent and an explanation of the transaction in lay terms, including the next steps. This will help SOCA and law enforcement to decide whether to grant consent in relation to POCA 2002, ss.327–329. Paragraph 8.3.7 of the AML practice note provides information on obtaining consent. The MLRO should print a copy of the report before submission to include in the legal practice's records.

The procedure will also cover what arrangements will be in place to cover the absence of the MLRO and the delegation of responsibility to the deputy MLRO.

6.4 After the report

The procedure (see **Annex 6A**) will set out what to do if consent is granted and how to handle clients during the period, including the fact that the MLRO will liaise with SOCA.

The procedure will also cover the situation where consent is refused and the approach during the 31-day moratorium period. Employees and managers/partners will need significant support during that period, which will be very difficult, particularly if the client has not consented to the report being made. Even where the report is made on behalf of the client, the client and the fee earner will need reassurance and support pending the decision by SOCA and law enforcement as to whether to take further action, e.g. to obtain a restraint order.

6.5 Using the toolkit

The internal reporting form (see **Annex 6B**) should be available to fee earners, preferably in the legal practice's AML manual.

The MLRO decision form (see **Annex 6C**) is useful for recording the decision-making process and summarising the information before using SAR Online. This will demonstrate that the MLRO has considered all the issues. The flow charts (see **Annex 6D**) will assist him or her in that analysis.

It is not suggested that the flow charts are disseminated to fee earners, as they may try to complete the forms themselves rather than seek guidance from the MLRO.

The procedure on responding to requests from law enforcement (see **Annex 6E**) is a general guide, but you should consider obtaining specialist legal advice, especially if the police are querying your involvement rather than seeking the file as part of the audit trail or querying the client's involvement.

Annex 6A
Procedure for making suspicious activity reports

Purpose

[*Legal practice name*] is committed to compliance with its AML/CTF obligations, in order to mitigate the risks of its services being used by money launderers or terrorist financers.

This procedure sets out how [*legal practice name*] will ensure that reports of suspicious activity are sent to and dealt with by the MLRO [and deputy MLRO].

Managers/partners or employees making reports

Where a manager/partner or employee has a suspicion of money laundering or terrorist financing, or is requested by the [deputy MLRO/MLRO] [or a manager/partner] to lodge a formal report following an initial request for guidance, he or she must complete an internal report form and send it to the [deputy MLRO/MLRO] at [*email address*].

The report must contain the key information requested in a concise manner.

The manager/partner or employee must cease acting on the relevant retainer except as authorised by the [deputy MLRO/MLRO] and must not discuss the retainer, the internal report or the external report except as authorised by the [deputy MLRO/MLRO].

The MLRO may also direct other equity managers/partners and employees who are working on other retainers for the client to cease acting on those retainers.

[Reports to deputy MLRO

The deputy MLRO is to review all internal reports to assess whether they require referral to the MLRO for a report to SOCA.

The deputy MLRO will authorise what further steps can be taken in respect of all relevant retainers and liaise with the relevant managers/partners and employees on what information can be communicated to the client. The employees and managers/partners must provide any further information requested by the deputy MLRO, who must have access to all information within [*legal practice name*] to enable decisions to be made about whether to report.

The deputy MLRO will review the report to consider the basis for suspicion and request further information and/or relevant enquiries to be made of the client or third parties promptly.]

Reports by the MLRO

The MLRO will review [all internal reports/all internal reports forwarded by the deputy MLRO] to consider the basis for suspicion and request further information and/or relevant enquiries to be made of the client or third parties promptly.

The MLRO will decide on the basis of his or her own assessment of the report and any further information whether to make a report to SOCA or terminate the retainer or both.

The MLRO will authorise what further steps can be taken in respect of any other retainers and liaise with the relevant managers/partners and employees on what information, if any, can be communicated to the client. The employees and managers/partners must provide any further information requested by the MLRO, who must have access to all information within [*legal practice name*] to enable decisions to be made about whether to report.

The MLRO will report to SOCA using the SAR Online reporting form and liaise with SOCA regarding any consent required under POCA 2002, ss.327, 328 or 329. The MLRO will advise the relevant employees and managers/partners as to how to handle the matter and the client subsequent to any report, including any issues arising while consent is awaited. This will include guidance on the tipping off offence in regulated sector cases and the prejudicing an investigation offences in all cases.

If consent is refused, the MLRO will liaise with the relevant managers/partners and employees as to what steps are to be taken.

Requests for information

If any requests for information are received from SOCA or other law enforcement agencies, such requests must immediately be passed to the [deputy MLRO/MLRO] in accordance with the procedure for responding to law enforcement requests.

Related policy

Anti-money laundering, counter-terrorist financing and sanctions compliance policy

Glossary

AML	anti-money laundering
consent	permission to proceed with a retainer even though there is a suspicion of money laundering
CTF	counter-terrorist financing
MLRO	money laundering reporting officer, also known as a nominated officer
POCA 2002	Proceeds of Crime Act 2002
SAR	suspicious activity report, also known as a disclosure
SOCA	Serious Organised Crime Agency

Date of effect/date of review

This procedure shall come into effect on [*date*]. This procedure shall be reviewed annually.

Annex 6B

Internal report form

Internal details	
Date:	File number:
Reporter:	Role:
Email:	Extension:

Client details	
Full name:	
Sex: M/F	Date of birth:
ID document type: ☐ Passport ☐ Drivers licence ☐ Other:	
Document number:	
Business name:	
Company number:	VAT number:
Address (including full postcode):	
Phone number:	
Acting as agent: Y/N	Acting as trustee: Y/N

Retainer details	
Describe the retainer:	
Explain the current stage of the retainer:	
Outline the next steps to be taken with time frames and the expected completion date:	

Details of person or entity suspected	
☐ Client ☐ Company employee ☐ Third party funder ☐ Counter party	
☐ Other:	
If client, proceed to **Basis for suspicion** section. For all others complete identity details below	
Name:	
Sex: M/F	Date of birth:
ID document type: ☐ Passport ☐ Drivers licence ☐ Other:	
Document number:	
Business name:	
Company number:	VAT number:

Address (including full postcode):	
Phone number:	
Acting as agent: Y/N	Acting as trustee: Y/N
Basis for suspicion	
Outline what it is you suspect (refer to the specific warning signs, identify the existing criminal property or give reasons for suspecting terrorist financing):	
Explain how you received this information:	
Outline any conversations you have already had with the client about the issues on which your suspicion is based:	
Outline any other information that you consider relevant to this report:	

Annex 6C
MLRO decision form

Date:	File number:

Reporter/practice area:

Background
Summarise the suspicion as reported to you:
Did the information on which the suspicion was based come to the legal practice in the course of business in the regulated sector? Y/N
Summarise any further enquiries undertaken and their results:

Decision taken
Do you have knowledge or suspicion of terrorist financing or money laundering? Y/N
If no, explain why not:
If yes, summarise the suspicion of terrorist financing or the suspicion or knowledge of existing criminal property:
Does privilege apply or did the information come in privileged circumstances? Y/N Explain why or why not:
Is there any other reason not to report which is permitted by law? Y/N If yes, provide the reason:
Does the legal practice require consent? Y/N
Does the client require consent? Y/N
Have you obtained instructions from the client to seek consent on his or her behalf? Y/N
Summarise what you need to seek consent to do:
Are there any other ethical or civil liability considerations which may warrant ceasing to act for the client? Y/N Explain why or why not:

Summarise the final decision made:

Report logistics
Making the report
Date of report:
Time:
Consent requested: Y/N
Other people authorised to discuss with SOCA or law enforcement:
Response from SOCA or law enforcement
Date of response:
Time:
What consent was granted: Y/N
Summarise any other requests for information or any information received:
Managing fee earner and client expectations
Summarise your instructions to the fee earner:
Summarise any further discussions with the client on this issue:

Annex 6D

Flow charts

Flow chart 1: Which reporting regime do I need to consider?

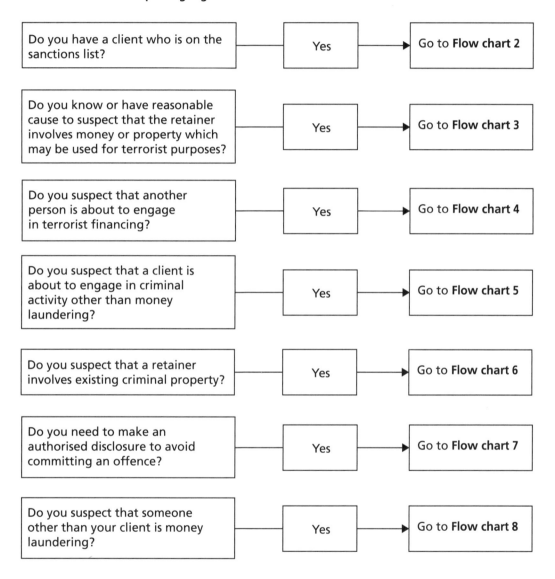

Do you have a client who is on the sanctions list?	Yes	Go to **Flow chart 2**
Do you know or have reasonable cause to suspect that the retainer involves money or property which may be used for terrorist purposes?	Yes	Go to **Flow chart 3**
Do you suspect that another person is about to engage in terrorist financing?	Yes	Go to **Flow chart 4**
Do you suspect that a client is about to engage in criminal activity other than money laundering?	Yes	Go to **Flow chart 5**
Do you suspect that a retainer involves existing criminal property?	Yes	Go to **Flow chart 6**
Do you need to make an authorised disclosure to avoid committing an offence?	Yes	Go to **Flow chart 7**
Do you suspect that someone other than your client is money laundering?	Yes	Go to **Flow chart 8**

Flow chart 2: The retainer involves a sanctioned entity

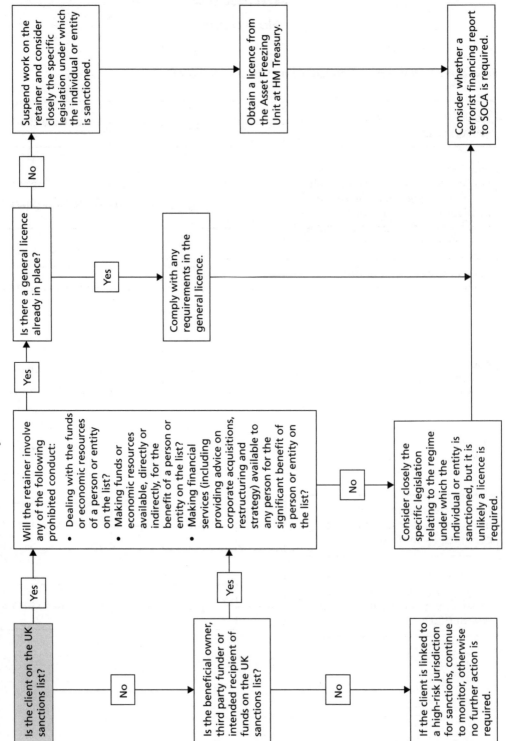

Flow chart 3: I suspect that the retainer involves money or property which may be used for terrorist purposes

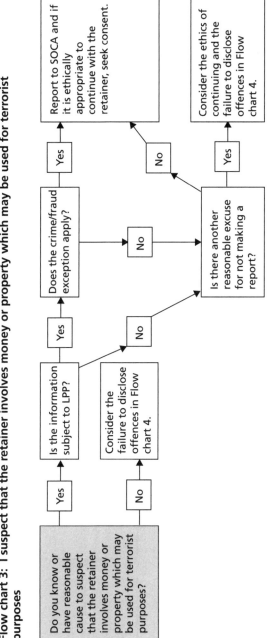

Flow chart 4: I suspect that another person is about to be engaged in terrorist financing

```
Is the
retainer in
the
regulated
sector?
        │
        ▼
Do you know or          ── No ──▶  No further action
have reasonable                    necessary unless
cause to suspect                   there are other
that another person                concerns.
is engaged in
terrorist financing?
        │
        │ Yes
        ▼
Is the information      ── Yes ──▶  Does the crime/      ── Yes ──▶  Report to SOCA.
subject to LPP?                     fraud exception
        │                           apply?
        │ No                            │
        ▼                               │ No
Is there another   ◀────────────────────┘
reasonable
excuse for not         ── No ──▶  Report to SOCA.
making a report?
        │
        │ Yes
        ▼
                        Consider ethics
                        of continuing.

Is the
retainer in
the
unregulated
sector?
        │
        ▼
Do you know or          ── No ──▶  No further action
suspect that another               necessary unless
person is engaged in               there are other
terrorist financing?               concerns.
        │
        │ Yes
        ▼
Is the information subject to LPP?
```

Flow chart 5: I suspect a client is about to engage in criminal activity other than money laundering

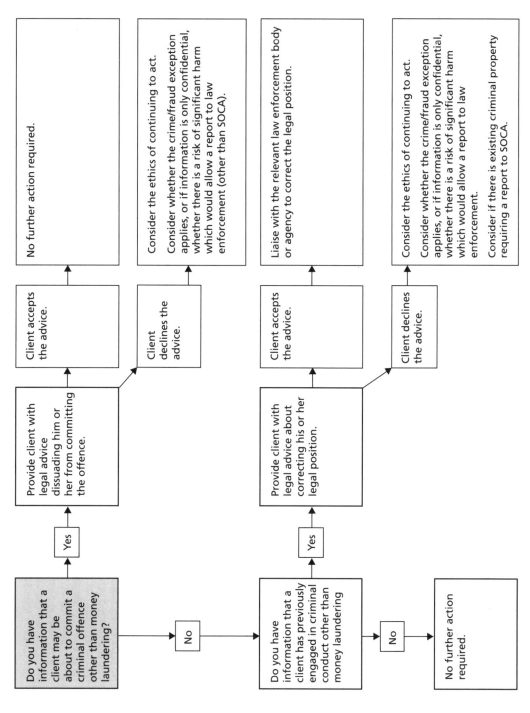

Flow chart 6: I suspect a client is about to engage in money laundering

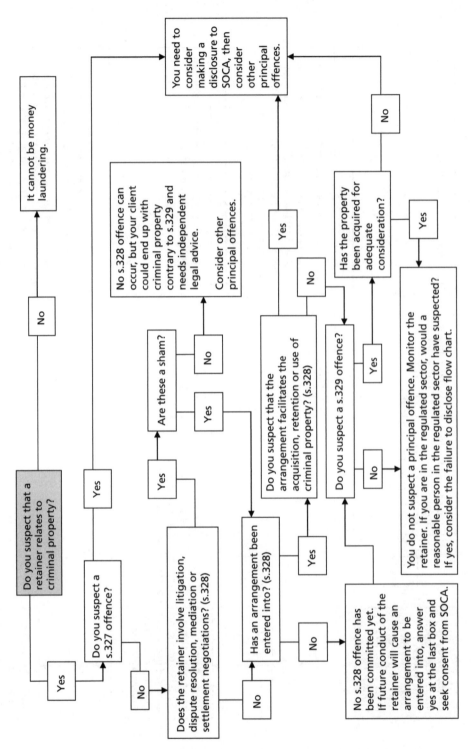

Flow chart 7: I suspect I may be involved in money laundering, do I need to make a disclosure?

Flow chart 8: I suspect someone else is money laundering, do I need to make a disclosure?

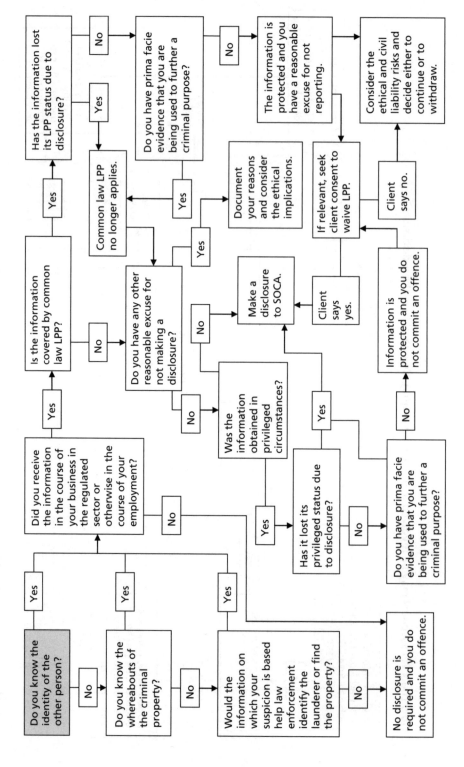

Annex 6E
Procedure for responding to law enforcement requests

Purpose

[*Legal practice name*] is committed to compliance with its AML/CTF obligations, in order to mitigate the risks of its services being used by money launderers or terrorist financers.

This procedure sets out how [*legal practice name*] will ensure that production orders or requests for information from law enforcement are responded to by the legal practice.

Application

This procedure applies to all staff in [*legal practice name*]. Failure to comply with this procedure [will/may] result in disciplinary action.

Requests for information from law enforcement, etc.

The employee is responsible for transferring any telephone call received from a police officer, SOCA officer or SFO officer requesting information, advising that a production order is to be served or indicating that a search warrant may be issued to the [MLRO/deputy MLRO/AML team].

The employee will advise the officer that the call will be transferred to the [MLRO/ deputy MLRO/AML team] and will then advise the [MLRO/deputy MLRO/AML team] of the name of the officer, the police force or organisation and the details of the case.

If the [MLRO/deputy MLRO/AML team] is not available, the employee will take the officer's details and advise that the [MLRO/deputy MLRO/AML team] will return the call within [*specify time frame, e.g. 24 hours*].

The employee is responsible for immediately forwarding any email or letter from a police officer, SOCA officer or SFO officer requesting information, advising that a production order is to be served or indicating that a search warrant may be issued to the [MLRO/deputy MLRO/AML team].

The employee will acknowledge receipt to the officer, advising that the email or letter will be forwarded to the [MLRO/deputy MLRO/AML team].

The employee must not confirm or deny any information or indicate whether or not [*legal practice name*] acts or has acted in the matter or for that client.

The [MLRO/deputy MLRO/AML team] will, on receipt of the telephone call, email or letter, ascertain from the officer the key details about the case, what information is requested or when the order will be served and whether it appears that the request or order will override the duty of confidentiality, e.g. if the order relates to a SAR.

The [MLRO/deputy MLRO/AML team] will be responsible for assessing whether and on what grounds the client should be advised of the request, and the implications and risks of doing so.

The [MLRO/deputy MLRO/AML team] will, in discussing the matter with the officer, without obstructing the investigation, determine whether there is any flexibility as to the length of time in which to provide the information or comply with the order.

The [MLRO/deputy MLRO/AML team] will advise the officer on whom the request or order is to be served and the relevant address, email and fax details. A hard-copy production order must always be served on [legal practice name] in addition to a fax.

The [MLRO/deputy MLRO/AML team] will contact the [fee earner/supervising partner/COLP/managing partner/board] to advise him or her of the request or order, providing the key details, including the timescale and whether there may be any concerns at this stage about [legal practice name]'s actions/involvement in the matter.

The [MLRO/deputy MLRO/AML team] will request the file from the fee earner or archive within [24 hours/two days].

Complying with the request or order

On receipt of the request for information or the production order, the [MLRO/ deputy MLRO/AML team] will assess its validity and provisions.

If the view of the [MLRO/deputy MLRO/AML team] is that the request or order is not valid, [he or she/it] will take [internal/external] legal advice and in accordance with that advice, challenge the request or order.

If the view of the [MLRO/deputy MLRO/AML team] is that the request or order gives rise to concerns about the position of [legal practice name], [he or she/it] will take [internal/external] legal advice and advise the [supervising partner/COLP/ managing partner/board] accordingly.

If the request, order or warrant appears valid and to override confidentiality, the [MLRO/deputy MLRO/AML team] is responsible for ensuring compliance with the request, order or warrant within the timescales, subject to other ethical considerations.

The [MLRO/deputy MLRO/AML team] will request such further information, including the relevant file, from the employee or manager/partner as is necessary to ensure compliance.

On receipt of the file, the [MLRO/deputy MLRO/AML team] will assess it and determine if there are concerns about the handling of the file and [assess the file for privileged material/seek [internal/external] advice on privileged material]. A copy of the file will be made and retained in place of the original file.

The employee or manager/partner must provide any further information requested by the [MLRO/deputy MLRO/AML team] as is necessary to ensure compliance.

On the basis of the advice or assessment, the privileged material will be removed from the file and marked as 'privileged', a sheet being placed in the original file to denote that fact. If part of a document is privileged, that part will be redacted. The redacted version will be placed on the original file and the original, duly annotated, will be placed on the copy file.

The [MLRO/deputy MLRO/AML team] will liaise with the officer to provide the file and deal with any subsequent enquiries.

The [MLRO/deputy MLRO/AML team] will authorise what further steps can be taken in respect of any current retainers and liaise with the relevant managers/partners and employees on what information, if any, can be communicated to the client.

This will include guidance on the tipping off offence in regulated sector cases and the prejudicing an investigation offences in all cases.

Related policy

Anti-money laundering, counter-terrorist financing and sanctions compliance policy

Glossary

AML	anti-money laundering
CTF	counter-terrorist financing
MLRO	money laundering reporting officer, also known as a nominated officer
SFO	Serious Fraud Office
SOCA	Serious Organised Crime Agency

Date of effect / date of review

This procedure shall come into effect on [*date*]. This procedure shall be reviewed annually.

7 Client exit strategy

Legal practices will consider carefully whether to continue acting for a client, where there are POCA or MLR concerns. Difficult decisions may need to be made by the MLRO and COLP which result in the termination of the retainer, despite commercial pressures.

Under MLR 2007, reg.11, if you cannot apply CDD measures in accordance with MLR 2007, you must:

- terminate any existing business relationship with the client; and
- consider whether you are required to make a disclosure under POCA 2002 or the Terrorism Act 2000.

For the following reasons you may also decide to cease acting or withdraw in the following situations:

- you have made a report under POCA 2002, s.330;
- you have reported under POCA 2002, s.327, 328 or 329 and received consent;
- you have strong prima facie evidence that you are being or have been used as an instrument of fraud but there is no suggestion of money laundering or terrorist financing;
- the information is covered by legal professional privilege or received in privileged circumstances and the crime/fraud exception does not apply;
- the degree of trust in confidentiality necessary between solicitor and client has been eroded.

There may be other reasons why you decide it is not appropriate to continue to act, for example, on ethical grounds or because of reputational risk.

Having reached the decision to cease acting, there are a number of issues to consider to minimise the risk of criticism from the client, the SRA or law enforcement, including:

- duties under the Code of Conduct;
- advising the client;
- allegations of discrimination;
- outstanding fees;
- reputational impact;
- potential civil liability;
- advising the other side.

The termination of a retainer is always difficult, but the added complication of offences under POCA 2002 and the Terrorism Act 2000 means that the termination needs to be carefully handled.

The legal practice's policy on termination of retainers is likely to cover the broader issues, e.g. conflicts of interests, reputational issues, ethical issues and liaison with the COLP.

7.1 Duties under the Code of Conduct

When deciding whether to terminate your instructions, you must comply with the law and the Code of Conduct (outcome 1.3) and consider the chapter 1 outcomes. You may also take into account outcomes and IBs in chapters 3, 4, 5 (if there is a court case), 10 and 11.

In reaching your decision, you will need to take into account IB 1.7, IB 1.10 and IB 1.26. Given that IB 1.10 is about explaining the client's possible options for pursuing the matter, it is helpful that IB 4.4 makes specific reference to the money laundering legislation. Due to the possible tension between those IBs and your legal obligations, it will be vital to document what actions you took and why, in consultation with the COLP.

7.2 Advising the client

Under outcome 1.1, you must treat your client fairly. You should ensure you have considered all the relevant issues, given the client the opportunity to provide explanations and, where appropriate, explained the implications of his or her course of action, bearing in mind that it is not tipping off to seek to dissuade a client from engaging in criminal conduct. You will need to consider the ethical issues and advise the client you are no longer able to act. You might say you are unable to act for professional reasons. The full reasons need to be documented on a separate POCA file. You may wish to copy the client file in case of follow-up queries, as the client will be entitled to the original file subject to any lien.

If no report to SOCA has been made, but you are terminating the retainer, the situation may be less complex provided that you do not know or suspect an investigation is being or is about to be conducted.

If you have decided to make a report under POCA 2002, s.330, you may consider ceasing to act first as that might make the termination less difficult, but you need to bear in mind s.333A(3).

The procedure should make it clear that no action is to be taken without guidance and approval from the MLRO, particularly given the complex tipping off provisions as well as those relating to prejudicing an investigation.

7.3 Allegations of discrimination

By documenting on the central POCA file the decision to cease acting and ensuring compliance with chapter 2 of the Code of Conduct and the legal practice's own equality and diversity policy, the legal practice can demonstrate that the decision to cease acting was not due to direct or indirect discrimination.

7.4 Outstanding fees

The legal practice will need to decide whether to pursue any fees. If monies are held on account, you should be able to retain those monies provided you comply with the SRA Accounts Rules 2011 and if the adequate consideration defence applies (see para.5.5.2 of the Law Society's AML practice note).

7.5 Reputational impact

There is a risk of reputational impact in ceasing to act, whether it is a high profile client or not. The client may make public comment about the termination and you may be restricted in what you can say due to confidentiality or because you have made a report. The client may complain to the Legal Ombudsman or the SRA. Guidance from the marketing team will be invaluable in ensuring that any reputational issues are identified at an early stage and then managed by the MLRO and the COLP.

7.6 Potential civil liability

In ceasing to act, you may consider whether you have acted as a constructive trustee and whether you are open to any potential civil liability. Chapter 10 of the Law Society's AML practice note will assist.

7.7 Advising the other side

The issues in advising the other side are similar to those in relation to the client. If you have made a report, you will need to consider the issues of tipping off and how you will advise the other side that you are no longer acting without putting them on notice that you have made a report.

As with most situations, the best approach is to keep it brief, but if the other side request further information, you will refer to your duty of confidentiality. It is unlikely that there will be any grounds for indicating to the other side why you are ceasing to act, even if you have concerns about their client. You cannot pass your client's details to the other side, due to your duty of confidentiality, but you can offer to pass a letter to your client.

7.8 Using the toolkit

The procedure for exiting a client relationship (see **Annex 7A**) is to assist fee earners and ensure that they do not take steps in isolation. There will have been guidance from and discussion with the MLRO before this point is reached, so the fee earner should not consider taking steps without further advice.

Annex 7A

Procedure for exiting client relationships

Purpose

[*Legal practice name*] is committed to compliance with its AML/CTF obligations, in order to mitigate the risks of its services being used by money launderers or terrorist financers.

This procedure sets out how [*legal practice name*] will ensure that the risks of the practice committing offences while exiting client relationships are minimised.

Application

This procedure applies to all staff in [*legal practice name*] and sets out the requirements for exiting the client relationship. Failure to comply with this procedure [will/may] result in disciplinary action.

Ceasing to act

Employees must cease acting for the client if the client's identity cannot be obtained within [*specify time frame, e.g. one month*] of receiving instructions or requesting further CDD information. Details must be provided to the [MLRO/AML team] who will decide whether to make a report to SOCA.

Employees must cease acting if directed to do so by the [MLRO/AML team/ managing partner/supervising partner] and must follow the directions of the [MLRO/AML team] in terminating the retainer. Those directions will [be made in liaison with the COLP and] cover the following issues, taking into account [*legal practice name*]'s termination of retainer policy:

- duties under the SRA Code of Conduct 2011;
- advising the client;
- allegations of discrimination;
- outstanding fees;
- reputational impact;
- potential civil liability;
- advising the other side.

Employees must make a detailed note of the instructions from the [MLRO/AML team] and the actions taken as a result, which must be placed on the [central] [departmental] POCA file. Such notes must not be placed on the client file. The [MLRO/AML team] will advise what information must be copied or retained before passing the file to the client or another legal practice, subject to any lien.

Employees must seek guidance from the [MLRO/AML team] if any queries are raised by the client.

No action is to be taken without guidance and approval from the MLRO, particularly given the complex tipping off provisions and those relating to prejudicing an investigation.

Allegations of discrimination

If the client raises any allegations of direct or indirect discrimination, immediate guidance must be sought from the [MLRO/AML team]. Employees are reminded of the need for compliance with chapter 2 of the SRA Code of Conduct 2011 and the legal practice's own equality and diversity policy.

Outstanding fees

If there are any outstanding fees, guidance must be sought from the [MLRO/AML team] as to what action is to be taken and whether to pursue any fees. The [MLRO/AML team] will take into account the obligations under the SRA Accounts Rules 2011 and whether the adequate consideration defence in POCA 2002, s.329 applies.

Reputational impact

If the client indicates that he or she may make any public comment or complain to the Legal Ombudsman or the SRA about the termination, guidance must be sought from the [MLRO/AML team] and the COLP, who will discuss the situation as appropriate with the marketing team to identify all issues at an early stage and manage such issues.

Potential civil liability

Where monies are held, employees and managers/partners must provide full details to the [MLRO/AML team] so an assessment can be made of whether [*legal practice name*] is acting as a constructive trustee and is open to any potential civil liability.

Advising the other side

Employees must follow the instructions of the [MLRO/AML team] in communicating with the other side to ensure that there are no breaches of the tipping off or prejudicing an investigation offences.

If the other legal party, or any other third party, seeks further information, guidance must be sought from the [MLRO/AML team]. Employees must not indicate why they are ceasing to act, even when they have concerns about the client of the other legal practice. Employees must not pass the client's details to the other side, due to the duty of confidentiality. The [MLRO/AML team] will advise whether the employee can offer to pass a letter to the client.

Related policies

- Anti-money laundering, counter-terrorist financing and sanctions compliance policy
- Termination of retainer policy
- Equality and diversity policy

Glossary

AML	anti-money laundering
CDD	client due diligence
COLP	compliance officer for legal practice
CTF	counter-terrorist financing
MLRO	money laundering reporting officer, also known as a nominated officer
POCA 2002	Proceeds of Crime Act 2002
SOCA	Serious Organised Crime Agency

Date of effect/date of review

This procedure shall come into effect on [date]. This procedure shall be reviewed annually.

PART 3
Making sure it all works

This section of the toolkit looks at the 'behind the scenes' work required to ensure that employees understand their obligations and the legal practice can demonstrate how it is complying with its obligations to prevent money laundering, terrorist financing and breaches of the sanctions regime.

8 Training

8.1 Why train?

Under MLR 2007, reg.21, you must take appropriate measures so that all relevant employees are:

(a) made aware of the law relating to money laundering and terrorist financing; and
(b) regularly given training in how to recognise and deal with transactions and other activities which may be related to money laundering or terrorist financing.

Failure to do so leaves the legal practice and its managers/partners open to criminal sanctions.

Under POCA 2002, s.330(7), staff will have a defence if they do not know or suspect money laundering and they have not been provided with training in relation to money laundering by their employer.

Under chapter 7 of the Code of Conduct, you must train your staff (outcome 7.6) and comply with anti-money laundering legislation (outcome 7.5).

Everyone in the legal practice must understand that undertaking the training is non-negotiable and that failure to undertake training will be escalated to the supervising partner, head of department or managing partner as well as having an impact on performance reviews, appraisal and, ultimately, salary.

8.2 Who to train?

If the legal practice has a conveyancing, corporate or trust and probate team, you will need to ensure that all new employees and managers/partners have basic knowledge about POCA 2002 and MLR 2007, including the CDD procedures. Such legal practices are then likely to provide some form of more detailed or refresher training specifically designed for those teams which focuses on the real risks and includes case studies.

If the legal practice verifies the identity of all clients, all staff need to be trained on the CDD procedures as well as POCA 2002.

You will also need to consider what training is required for accounts staff, whose perspective is different from that of fee earners. They need to know how to spot transactions of potential concern and raise questions with fee earners, particularly if funds are received from unusual sources.

Reception staff will need to know how to deal with clients arriving with cash or identification documents and the procedure to follow if the police arrive with a production order.

Other staff, e.g. the personal injury team in a legal practice which does not verify the identity of personal injury clients, or staff in other support functions, may simply need basic training on the law, who the MLRO is and where to go for help. It is important to ensure that those staff have sufficient knowledge to spot potential money laundering.

8.3 What type of training?

Paragraph 3.9 of the Law Society's AML practice note provides guidance on training and what to consider. There is a range of training options available, from face-to-face training to online desk-based training. Legal practices should consider their risk profile and training needs before deciding on the most appropriate mechanism. The advice and support of the HR or training team will be vital to successful implementation.

You will need to decide how often to train staff. The general view is that staff should be trained every two years. However, the obligation is to give relevant staff regular training, so you will decide what is appropriate for the legal practice's risk profile in order to protect the staff and the managers/partners.

Online training may provide the base level of training. Such systems ensure that not only do you know what training everyone has undertaken, but also allow you to identify those that have not undertaken any training. An advantage of online training is that it can be undertaken at the desk, reducing time away from fee-earning work. An online training system can be a powerful tool which may allow you to:

- record the details of the individual, including his or her status, department, SRA number, date of joining, etc.;
- allocate different courses to different teams;
- report which individuals have done the training and their assessment results;
- report who has not done the training;
- send reminders to those who have not done the training;
- link the training system with the continuing professional development (CPD) reporting system.

Face-to-face training will ensure that employees can interact with the trainer and ask questions. They may also be more engaged, especially if it is clear that the training has been planned by the MLRO and the head of the department. It is an opportunity to ask employees to apply the legal practice's procedures to practical scenarios based on real-life cases. Discussing the challenges of obtaining information about source of funds as part of ongoing monitoring as well as what 'consistent with the risk profile' means may be of real value to fee earners. The success of the training can be measured by the number of queries that the MLRO receives!

Other forms of training for staff may include discussions at team meetings, circulation of relevant articles or bulletins, participation in dedicated AML/CTF forums and access to an up-to-date AML manual as a reference source between training sessions.

You will also need to consider how to keep employees up to date with emerging risks and developments in the law.

It would be prudent to make notes about your assessment of training needs, how they are being addressed and why the training has been assessed as effective.

8.4 Records

You must have a record of the training provided, not only for CPD purposes but also to demonstrate compliance to the SRA and law enforcement. It will also enable you to refute any allegation by an employee that you have not provided training under either MLR 2007 or POCA 2002.

8.5 Using the toolkit

The training procedure (see **Annex 8A**) will set out the details of the training that will be provided to the legal practice and this should be easily accessible to all employees. The training delivery log (see **Annex 8B**) provides a record of the training; a copy of the training materials should also be retained.

Annex 8A
Training procedure

Purpose

[*Legal practice name*] is committed to compliance with its AML/CTF obligations, in order to mitigate the risks of its services being used by money launderers or terrorist financers.

This procedure sets out how [*legal practice name*] will train staff to minimise the risk of [*legal practice name*] being used by money launderers or terrorist financers and how that information will be recorded.

Application

[*Delete as appropriate:*]

[This procedure applies to all staff in [*legal practice name*].]

[This procedure applies to the [MLRO/deputy MLRO/AML team] and relevant staff in [*legal practice name*] as set out below [*delete as appropriate*]:

- all partners and fee earners;
- all support staff;
- all accounts staff;
- all partners and fee earners in the regulated sector;
- all support staff in the regulated sector;
- [*specify other*]]

Failure to comply with this procedure [will/may] result in disciplinary action.

Training for the MLRO

The MLRO is responsible for ensuring that he or she [, the deputy MLRO and the AML team] stay[s] up to date on AML/CTF law and practice.

The MLRO [, the deputy MLRO and the AML team] will undertake formal training [annually/every six months] by way of attending seminars or networking groups or completing online training.

The MLRO [, the deputy MLRO and the AML team] will also subscribe to and read:

- the Law Society's bi-monthly AML e-newsletter;
- [*specify any other relevant publications*].

Provision of training to the legal practice

The MLRO is responsible for preparing an AML/CTF training plan for [*legal practice name*] [annually/every six months].

The [HR/training/learning and development] team is required to assist the [MLRO/ deputy MLRO/AML team] in providing the training, recording the training and ensuring that CPD records are kept up to date.

[The training plan will be agreed with the relevant area managers/partners.]

[*Delete as appropriate:*]

[Formal training will be provided by way of seminars or online training to all staff (other than the MLRO [, deputy MLRO and AML team]) [every two years/every 18 months/annually/every six months].]

[Formal training will be provided by way of seminars or online training to all relevant staff as set out below:]

Staff group	Frequency

Formal training will cover the warning signs of money laundering and terrorist financing relevant to the legal practice and practice area and the steps required to be taken by staff to comply with the law in accordance with the procedures of [*legal practice name*].

The [MLRO/deputy MLRO/AML team] is responsible for providing AML/CTF alerts to all [relevant] staff on warning signs, current methodologies or relevant changes to practice.

Training on recognising warning signs, conducting risk assessments, undertaking CDD and making internal reports will be provided to all [relevant] staff on induction and transfer between departments.

If a supervisor becomes aware of a significant gap in a [relevant] staff member's knowledge he or she will notify the [MLRO/deputy MLRO/AML team].

The MLRO may require any [relevant] staff member or practice area to undertake additional AML/CTF training where he or she believes it is necessary to ensure compliance with AML/CTF obligations.

Responsibilities of [relevant] staff

All [relevant] staff must attend, participate in and complete such training and achieve the necessary pass mark as is required by [*legal practice name*] within the required timescale.

Failure to do so may be noted on the individual's performance review or appraisal and may result in disciplinary action.

Record of the training

Details of the training will be recorded for CPD purposes and to demonstrate compliance with MLR 2007 and the SRA Code of Conduct 2011.

Training will be recorded on the attached form [and/or] in the Law Society CPD centre.

Related policy

Anti-money laundering, counter-terrorist financing and sanctions compliance policy

Glossary

AML	anti-money laundering
CDD	client due diligence
CPD	continuing professional development
CTF	counter-terrorist financing
MLR 2007	Money Laundering Regulations 2007
MLRO	money laundering reporting officer, also known as a nominated officer

Date of effect/date of review

This procedure shall come into effect on [date]. This procedure shall be reviewed annually.

Annex 8B
Training delivery log

Date of training	Fee earner/ status	Department	Title of training	Type of training (e.g. online)	Materials used (e.g. handouts)	Trainer	Summary of test results (pass/fail)

9 Record-keeping

Regulation 19 of MLR 2007 requires legal practices to keep certain records about clients. Failure to do so leaves the legal practice and the managers/partners open to criminal prosecution under reg.45, as well as regulatory sanctions from the SRA.

Under reg.20, legal practices 'must establish and maintain appropriate and risk-sensitive policies and procedures' in relation to AML/CTF and so records are needed to show that these policies and procedures are in place. The key areas are:

- CDD measures and ongoing monitoring;
- reporting;
- record-keeping;
- internal control;
- risk assessment and management;
- the monitoring of compliance with the policies and procedures;
- the internal communication of the policies and procedures.

Systems need to be in place to hold records for the right period and in an appropriate and easily accessible format in order to demonstrate the legal practice's compliance to the SRA and law enforcement.

The precise nature of the records is not specified and reg.19 is not easy to follow. However, the defence in reg.45(4) is that the legal practice has taken all reasonable steps and exercised all due diligence to avoid committing the offence. The key elements of reg.45 relate to CDD and ongoing monitoring measures, enhanced due diligence, record-keeping and policies and procedures.

Whatever systems you use, you will need appropriate back-up systems (see IB 7.3 of the Code of Conduct) so you can then demonstrate to the SRA and law enforcement that you hold the necessary records. If you cannot show you ever held the records, law enforcement and the SRA may take the view that you never obtained the information, e.g. identification. Equally, an incomplete or inadequate record will leave you open to criticism. You must be able to produce the records without delay.

You will need to balance MLR 2007 obligations with those under the Data Protection Act 1998, so only keep the information that is necessary and ensure it is accurate and kept up to date.

9.1 What records must be kept?

Legal practices need to have proper and complete records in a format that can be easily accessed. Your procedure will set out the details of what records must be kept and for how long. The procedure needs to be compatible with or part of the legal practice's document retention policy or procedure.

Failure to comply with these obligations could expose the individual to disciplinary sanctions and could be a criminal matter.

You will retain the CDD documents initially obtained and also the supporting records (either original documents or copies) obtained for ongoing monitoring. Any supporting records may be contained in good file notes about the transaction but must be accessible, e.g. in an electronic file. An electronic record of the fact that identification has been obtained and the date it was obtained enables a legal practice to monitor compliance. You will also need to retain risk assessment notes (see para.3.8.2 of the Law Society's AML practice note).

Your procedure should cover enhanced CDD measures applied on a risk-sensitive basis as part of good case management, bearing in mind the comments at **4.6**. You need to demonstrate to the SRA that the extent of the measures is appropriate in view of the risks. Proper records of your decision-making process will assist.

Fee earners should note key issues and concerns about a client on the file as part of good case management and raise any queries with the MLRO. Reminding staff of the critical need to keep informative, accurate, legible and contemporaneous file notes will help to embed the right culture and demonstrate that you 'know your client'.

You must record particular transactions but, provided you comply with the SRA Accounts Rules 2011, you will have the information recorded elsewhere, particularly on the client ledger and supporting documents. Those records should enable a financial investigator (with a production order) to follow the financial audit trail.

The AML practice note, at para.3.8.4, provides guidance on what records to keep in relation to reports of suspicious activities, both internal and external.

Your record of training should include the information about who has been trained, when and how, so you can demonstrate compliance. This will also help to protect the legal practice against any allegations that training has not been provided under MLR 2007, reg.21 or POCA 2002, s.330(7). You may also include an assessment of the effectiveness of the training and how it meets the training needs identified.

Records of compliance monitoring should link to your compliance plan, as agreed with the COLP. A compliance monitoring log is found at **Annex 10B**.

The policies and procedures relating to internal control, risk assessment and management as well as internal communication will form the relevant records provided they are written, kept up to date (with version control) and communicated to all staff.

9.2 How long must you keep the records?

Under MLR 2007, records must be kept for five years but the variable is the starting point. Under reg.19, you must keep a copy of, or the references to, the evidence of identity obtained pursuant to regs.7, 8 and 14 for five years from the date on which the business relationship ends or the occasional transaction is completed.

You must also keep the supporting records for CDD or ongoing monitoring for five years:

- where the records relate to a particular transaction, from the date on which the transaction completed;
- for all other records, from the date on which the relationship ends.

You may decide to keep records for longer than five years, for example, if your document retention policy requires records to be kept for six years. Your procedure will take account of the requirements of the Data Protection Act 1998.

9.3 Where should you keep the records?

A prudent approach is to keep evidence of identification and CDD measures centrally so the information is accessible by other teams in the legal practice and can be provided to the SRA or law enforcement. Some legal practices will store the evidence electronically and others will hold a central register of information. Further guidance is at para.3.8.1 of the AML practice note.

In deciding where and how to keep the records, you may need to consider copyright issues and database/data protection issues.

9.4 Using the toolkit

The record-keeping procedure (see **Annex 9A**) will need to be available to all staff, who need to understand their obligations and the importance of keeping accurate and up-to-date records.

Annex 9A

Record-keeping procedure

Purpose

[*Legal practice name*] is committed to compliance with its AML/CTF obligations, in order to mitigate the risks of its services being used by money launderers or terrorist financers.

This procedure sets out how [*legal practice name*] will comply with its record-keeping obligations under MLR 2007.

Application

This procedure applies to all staff in [*legal practice name*] and sets out the requirements for record-keeping. Failure to comply with this procedure [will/may] result in disciplinary action.

Which records must be kept?

The following records must be kept:

- a copy of, or the references to, the evidence of the client's identity, plus supporting records (i.e. copies of original documents) obtained at client inception;
- a copy of, or the references to, the evidence of the client's identity, plus supporting records (i.e. copies of original documents) obtained as a result of ongoing monitoring;
- a copy of, or the references to, the relevant CDD information for beneficial owners;
- a copy of, or the references to, supporting records (either original documents or copies) of a business relationship or occasional transaction which is the subject of CDD or ongoing monitoring;
- documentary evidence about the nature and purpose of the retainer to comply with MLR 2007, reg.5(c) if you are in a business relationship;
- a copy of the risk assessment of the client, plus supporting records;
- documentary evidence of enhanced due diligence, including for PEPs;
- details of transactions [as set out in the accounting procedures] plus supporting documents;
- details of any concerns about the client or retainer;
- risk assessment profile of [*legal practice name*];
- records of AML/CTF training provided by [*legal practice name*];
- records of compliance monitoring;
- records of internal and external reports of suspicions or disclosures.

Staff must ensure that they comply with the client verification policy and the risk assessment policy and keep proper, accurate and complete records in accordance with this procedure.

An electronic record of the fact that identification has been obtained and the date will be kept on the [accounting system/central register].

[Where [*legal practice name*] has given consent to be relied on, the records will be made available [on request/as soon as is reasonably practicable].]

The record of the risk assessment profile of [*legal practice name*] will be maintained by the MLRO.

The training records will be maintained by the [MLRO/AML team/HR team/ training team].

The records of compliance monitoring will be kept by the [internal audit team/ MLRO/AML team].

The records of internal and external reports will be maintained by the [MLRO/ AML team].

For how long must the records be kept?

The identification and supporting records will be kept for [five/six] years from the date on which the occasional transaction is completed or the business relationship ends.

The records for each transaction will be kept for [five/six] years from the date on which the transaction is completed [as set out in the accounting procedures].

The training records will be kept for [five/six] years after the training is completed.

The records of compliance monitoring will be kept for [five/six] years.

The records of internal and external reports will be kept for [five/six] years.

[The records will be kept in accordance with the timescales set out in the document retention policy.]

Where will the records be kept?

The records will be held [by the library/in the central register/electronically].

What are your responsibilities?

[Fee earners/Secretaries] must record the information set out above. Training on the importance of such records has been provided to all staff, who must attend and participate in such training.

Queries about records

If a fee earner, employee or member of the accounts staff has a concern or a query about any aspect of the record-keeping obligations, he or she must contact the [MLRO/AML team], providing his or her details and details of the client, matter number, type of retainer and nature of the query.

The MLRO will record those details on the [attached/relevant] form and provide appropriate guidance, recording what advice was provided and when and how it was provided.

Related policies

- Anti-money laundering, counter-terrorist financing and sanctions compliance policy
- Document retention policy
- Accounting policies

Glossary

AML	anti-money laundering
CDD	client due diligence
CTF	counter-terrorist financing
MLR 2007	Money Laundering Regulations 2007
MLRO	money laundering reporting officer, also known as a nominated officer
PEP	politically exposed person

Date of effect/date of review

This procedure shall come into effect on [*date*]. This procedure shall be reviewed annually.

10 Monitoring compliance

Under MLR 2007, reg.20, the legal practice must have policies and procedures in place for managing and monitoring compliance with its AML obligations. Monitoring compliance enables you to assess whether the AML policies and procedures are effective. The COLP and the MLRO will liaise to ensure that the AML monitoring programme fits with that of the legal practice. The relevant elements will feed into the legal practice's compliance plan.

The key elements of any monitoring programme are to:

(a) identify whether the current procedures are being complied with;
(b) ensure relevant staff are aware of and understand the procedures;
(c) identify any compliance failings;
(d) identify any gaps in procedures;
(e) identify corrective actions;
(f) communicate the issues to the relevant people, e.g. the board, supervising partner or COLP;
(g) ensure follow-up actions and improvements to the systems are undertaken.

A compliance monitoring programme may include:

• file audits;
• file checklists to use before opening or closing a file;
• review of queries from staff;
• the MLRO's log of queries;
• reports made;
• reports from the MLRO to senior management on compliance;
• how to rectify any identified breaches of compliance and how improvements will be communicated to staff and fed back into the risk profile of the legal practice.

Your programme should be appropriate and proportionate for your legal practice, taking into account your overall risk profile, size of practice and type of client/work undertaken.

10.1 Compliance monitoring programme

The monitoring programme will review the effectiveness of the policies and procedures listed in MLR 2007, reg.20. The compliance monitoring form at **Annex 10B** provides examples of documents and systems to monitor.

Legal practices may find file reviews or internal or external audits are effective methods of monitoring compliance. Follow-up action can then be taken to remedy any failures and ensure that the procedures are tightened up.

Feedback and follow-up are critical to a successful monitoring programme. A written report can be circulated to relevant managers/partners, e.g. the supervising partner, setting out the corrective actions. The legal practice's procedure will cover the escalation process if corrective actions are not completed. The MLRO may need to take further action, e.g. provide training or revise procedures.

By reviewing both SARs and non-disclosures, you can assess whether the reporting procedure is working effectively and identify the reporting trends and any problems or risks. Responses from SOCA will inform this assessment.

10.2 Annual report

A prudent approach is for the MLRO to submit an annual report to the board (see **Annex 10C**) so they can assess whether the legal practice's AML systems and controls are operating effectively. The legal practice should determine the depth and frequency of information that is necessary.

The board should consider the report and take any necessary action to remedy any deficiencies identified in a timely manner. The report is likely to include whether there are sufficient resources to protect the legal practice, the outcomes of any internal or external audit reviews of the AML/CTF procedures as well as the outcome of any review of the risk assessment procedures.

The MLRO will tailor the report to the risk profile, size and nature of the legal practice. The key elements of the report are that it should review the effectiveness of the legal practice's systems and controls and make recommendations for improvement in the management of risks and priorities, including the allocation of resources. Some elements may not be relevant or appropriate for your legal practice.

The report should allow the MLRO to set out his or her duties, take stock of the year, plan work going forward, document key AML performance and risk indicators, record the policies in place and identify key issues that should be reported to senior management.

10.3 Using the toolkit

The procedure for monitoring compliance (see **Annex 10A**) will need to be accessible to staff so that they are clear about what is expected of them and to the internal audit team or external auditors so it is clear what has to be audited and the procedure for follow-up.

The compliance monitoring form (see **Annex 10B**) contains the issues to monitor. Legal practices will need to adapt the form to the needs of their business.

Annex 10A
Procedure for monitoring compliance

Purpose

[*Legal practice name*] is committed to compliance with its AML/CTF obligations, in order to mitigate the risks of its services being used by money launderers or terrorist financers.

This procedure sets out how [*legal practice name*] will ensure that the effectiveness of [*legal practice name*]'s policies and procedures will be monitored.

Application

This procedure applies to all staff in [*legal practice name*], who must comply with this procedure and complete any corrective actions identified.

The [internal audit team/external auditors] will undertake the monitoring of the AML systems in accordance with the [internal/external] audit process and this procedure and liaise with the [MLRO/AML team] and the COLP.

Failure to comply with this procedure [will/may] result in disciplinary action.

Compliance monitoring

Employees must cooperate with requests from the internal audit team to provide files and other information to enable the [internal/external] audit team to assess whether:

- identity checks have been completed as required by the client verification procedure;
- file opening checklists have been completed;
- satisfactory evidence of identity and source of funds has been obtained;
- risk assessments have been completed as required by the procedure;
- ongoing monitoring is being undertaken as required by the procedure;
- potential money laundering concerns have been raised with the [MLRO/AML team];
- reports have been made to the [MLRO/AML team];
- there have been any compliance failings.

Employees and managers/partners must respond promptly to further requests for information and acknowledge receipt of the report from the [internal/external] audit team. Employees and managers/partners must complete any corrective actions within [*specify time frame, e.g. one month*] of the report. Failure to respond promptly to requests for information, acknowledge receipt of the report or to complete corrective actions will result in a referral to the [MLRO/managing partner/COLP] for further action.

The [internal/external] audit team and the [MLRO/AML team/COLP] will review the [internal/external] audit results and decide what action is required to rectify any non-compliance. The [MLRO/AML team/COLP] will consider how improvements will be communicated to staff and fed back into the risk profile of the legal practice.

The [MLRO/AML team] will review SARs and non-disclosures to assess whether the reporting procedure is working effectively and identify the reporting trends and any problems or risks.

Provision of report to management

The MLRO will provide a report to the [management board/partnership/*other*] on [*legal practice name*]'s compliance with its AML/CTF obligations [every six months/annually].

The [board/partnership/*other*] will consider the report and take any necessary action to remedy any deficiencies identified within [*specify time frame, e.g. one month*].

The report will include an update on the following information for the reporting period:

* the training provided to managers/partners and employees on AML/CTF compliance and the names of any managers/partners or employees who did not attend such training;
* any material changes to AML/CTF risk factors affecting [*legal practice name*];
* details of any PEPs or other high-risk clients taken on by [*legal practice name*];
* the number of retainers terminated as a result of AML/CTF concerns or lack of CDD material;
* the number of internal reports made to the [MLRO or deputy MLRO/AML team];
* the number of external reports made by the MLRO or deputy MLRO;
* any response by SOCA or law enforcement to the SARs made;
* any other approaches by SOCA or law enforcement relating to AML/CTF concerns;
* any discussions with the SRA relating to AML/CTF concerns;
* any civil claims or notifications to insurers regarding AML/CTF issues;
* the results of any file audits or other monitoring activities of AML/CTF compliance within [*legal practice name*].

Related policy

Anti-money laundering, counter-terrorist financing and sanctions compliance policy

Glossary

AML	anti-money laundering
CDD	client due diligence
COLP	compliance officer for legal practice
CTF	counter-terrorist financing
MLRO	money laundering reporting officer, also known as a nominated officer
PEP	politically exposed person
SAR	suspicious activity report, also known as a disclosure
SOCA	Serious Organised Crime Agency
SRA	Solicitors Regulation Authority

Date of effect/date of review

This procedure shall come into effect on [*date*]. This procedure shall be reviewed annually.

Annex 10B
Compliance monitoring form

Type of monitoring	Date of monitoring	Key results/ concerns	Follow-up action	Date completed	Included in annual report
CDD					
CDD records					
Review of AML ID queries					
WIP report					
PEP register review					
[Reliance review]					
Ongoing monitoring review					
File reviews					
Internal/external audit results					
Reporting					
Review of internal reports					
Review of external reports					
Review of trends					
Review of SOCA liaison					
Record-keeping					
Review of records of CDD					
Review of records of transactions					
Internal controls					
Review of systems					
Review of AML manual					
Review of policies					
Review of cash payments					
Review of queries from accounts staff					

Type of monitoring	Date of monitoring	Key results/ concerns	Follow-up action	Date completed	Included in annual report
Risk assessment					
Review of risk assessments					
Review of guidance requests					
Training					
Training delivery log					
Training attendance report					
Communication					
Review of communications issued					
Discussion of AML at team meeting					

Annex 10C
MLRO report to management

Executive summary
1.   [*AML structure and governance*]
2.   [*Summary of business issues*]
3.   [*Report on procedures and policies*]
4.   [*Conclusions and recommendations*]
1.   **AML structure and governance**
1.1   Name of the MLRO, where based, employment dates and experience:
1.2   Name of any deputy:
1.3   Reporting lines and link to COLP:
1.4   Summary of MLRO's responsibilities including extent of any delegations:
1.5   MLRO functions, including responsibilities, resources (and whether sufficient) and any restrictions on fulfilling the role:
1.6   Name of nominated officer if different, or confirm that MLRO is the nominated officer:
1.7   When the report will be considered and by whom in senior management:
2.   **Summary of business issues**

2.1   Overview of the legal practice:
    • [*Numbers and types of staff, practice areas, types of work*]
    • [*Major areas of risk, with reference to the risk assessment of the legal practice*]
    • [*Client demographic/type*]
    • [*Source of funds, e.g. personal injury damages*]

2.2   Key strategic changes which will impact on the AML controls: • [*e.g. mergers*]

2.3   Other operational changes or other relevant issues:
    • [*New services*]
    • [*New systems, e.g. IT*]
    • [*Implementation*]
    • [*Improvements*]

2.4	Clients and CDD processes:

- *[What processes are used and by whom, e.g. central client inception team]*
- *[Size and type of client base by practice area/team]*
- *[Changes in client base, e.g. increase in foreign clients]*
- *[PEP policies and procedures and numbers of known PEPs]*
- *[Sanctions compliance processes]*
- *[Summary of checks, e.g. who, how, how often]*
- *[Procedures for third party verification/reliance]*
- *[Procedures for high-risk clients]*
- *[Systems for ongoing monitoring]*
- *[Systems for ensuring compliance and monitoring compliance]*

2.5	Types of services:

- *[Range of services]*
- *[Jurisdictions in which the legal practice operates and the risks]*
- *[How the services are provided and the risks]*

2.6	Record-keeping:

- *[Format and location of records]*
- *[Any material failures and corrective action taken]*

2.7	Production orders/law enforcement requests:

- *[Numbers and brief circumstances of orders served]*
- *[Lessons learnt]*

3	**Report on procedures and policies**

3.1	Overview of policies and procedures:

- *[Availability of policies and procedures]*
- *[AML manual]*
- *[How policies, etc. are communicated to staff]*

3.2	Training:

- *[Summary of training policy]*
- *[Training statistics for previous year]*
- *[Training provided (and to whom) in the previous year]*
- *[Training for MLRO and senior management, where different]*
- *[Evaluation of effectiveness]*
- *[Proposed training programme for next year including any budgetary issues]*
- *[Challenges in providing satisfactory and effective training and proposed solutions]*

3.3	Senior management information: • [*Arrangements for regular reporting, frequency and identifying to whom reports are made*] • [*Scope and coverage of regular reports*]
3.4	Policies and procedures • [*Effectiveness of policies and procedures, e.g. results of internal audits*] • [*Compliance failings*] • [*Corrective action*] • [*Changes to policies, etc. and why*]
3.5	Monitoring arrangements • [*Systems and controls to cover MLR 2007 obligations*] • [*Monitoring of systems and controls*] • [*Monitoring failings*] • [*Corrective action*] • [*Improvements to monitoring arrangements*]
3.6	Reporting • [*Review of systems to identify SARs*] • [*Number of internal reports made and by which practice area*] • [*Reasons for not reporting to SOCA*] • [*Number of external reports*] • [*Reporting trends*] • [*Feedback from SOCA on reports*] • [*Proposed improvements to systems*]
3.7	External factors • [*Use of Law Society updates*] • [*Impact of recent cases*] • [*Use of Financial Action Task Force guidance*] • [*Use of SOCA reports/threat assessments*] • [*Proposed regulatory/legislative changes*] • [*Impact of external factors on policy and risk management*] • [*Proposed or potential changes to policies and procedures*]

4	**Conclusions and recommendations**

4.1 Overall assessment of systems and controls

- *[Are they proportionate and comprehensive?]*
- *[Have they been regularly reviewed?]*
- *[Material control failures, liaison with COLP, issues identified and remedial action taken]*
- *[Effectiveness of monitoring processes]*
- *[Adequacy of resources]*

4.2 Recommendations for action

- *[Priorities for remedial action]*
- *[Time frame]*
- *[Resources required]*
- *[Potential impact of no action]*
- *[Other recommendations]*